Sigmund Freud Revisited

Twayne's World Authors Series

German Literature

David O'Connell, Editor

Georgia State University

TWAS 885

FREUD AT ABOUT FIFTY
(Sigmund Freud Archives, Inc., Library of Congress)

Sigmund Freud Revisited

Richard W. Noland

University of Massachusetts, Amherst

Twayne Publishers
New York

Twayne's World Authors Series No. 885
Sigmund Freud Revisited

Richard W. Noland

Twayne Publishers
1633 Broadway
New York, NY 10019

Library of Congress Cataloging-in-Publication Data

Noland, Richard W.
Sigmund Freud revisited / Richard W. Noland.
p. cm. — (Twayne's world authors series ; ISSN TWAS 885. German literature)
Includes bibliographical references (p.).
ISBN 0-8057-1684-X (alk. paper)
1. Freud, Sigmund, 1856–1939. 2. Psychoanalysts—Austria—Biography. I. Title. II. Series: Twayne's world authors series ; TWAS 885. III. Series: Twayne's world authors series. German literature.
BF109.F74N65 1999
150.19'52'092—dc21 99-29542
CIP

This paper meets the requirements of ANSI/NISO Z3948-1992 (Permanence of Paper).

10 9 8 7 6 5 4 3 2 1

Printed in the United States of America

To Barbara, and to Bill,
who at two broke Dr. Freud and has never forgotten it.

Contents

Preface

This book is an introduction to the life and work of Sigmund Freud. Though undergraduates and graduate students in psychology may find it useful, I have not primarily addressed it to a professional or preprofessional audience. I am not myself a psychologist and do not presume that I can instruct people who are far more knowledgeable in this field than I can ever be. More generally, however, I don't think that an understanding of Freud should be limited to a purely professional knowledge. Like Darwin and Marx, he is one of the supreme makers of the modern mind. He is worth the attention of anyone interested in the cultural life of the twentieth century. Accordingly, I have imagined an educated reader who knows something of Freud's influence on this century, who has a limited knowledge of what he actually said, and who would like to learn more about the man and his work.

My presentation is chronological, which I think is the best way to study Freud. His ideas do not appear as a finished whole from the beginning. They evolve over a very long time. Some basic ideas are present from the first, of which some continue unchanged to the end of his life and some change considerably. Others appear only as Freud encounters new clinical data or problems that must then be accommodated to or change the earlier ideas. In the course of this development many terms are redefined while others appear as new additions to his thinking. To read Freud properly, then, is to follow the development of his ideas, to follow his continuing and changing use of theoretical and clinical concepts, and to encounter the provisional nature of many of his formulations.

My emphasis is on Freud as a scientist and as a physician trying to help sick patients. That is how he begins, and he never ceases to emphasize the importance of intellectual scrutiny of observations, rather than revelation or intuition, as a source of knowledge. I do not mean that Freud cannot and should not be read as a thinker rather than as a scientist-doctor—as a twentieth-century philosopher, for example, who attempts to extend the Enlightenment program of the conquest of unreason by reason, as a romantic continuing the effort of earlier romantics to liberate humankind from the sterilities of reason and science, or as the originator of a new science of subjectivity that is both art and science. Still, Freud thinks of himself as a scientist and describes psychoanalysis as a science of the unconscious. I take him at his word on both of these points.

Of course, the scientific status of Freud—and of psychoanalysis—has been problematic from the beginning and continues to be for many people at the present time. Both inside and outside psychoanalysis, critics have challenged most of his basic ideas as well as many of his therapeutic claims. Thus, to revisit Freud in the 1990s is to encounter a man whose apparently assured scientific and cultural position is uncertain, to say the least. Freud bashing has become a popular sport in the last 20 years, and many of the bashers have no less as their aim than to remove Freud and psychoanalysis from the cultural scene. Both his life and his work are the target, depending on the critic and his or her special interest. In a work of the length of this study it is impossible to address fully all of these critical claims. I have, however, included a representative selection of such criticisms in the selected bibliography, including many of the most hostile on both his life and work. But I do not attempt to deal with each of these critics in a systematic way. That would lead to a study of twice the length of this book. I do, however, deal with some of the issues raised by these critics—for example, the issue of the truth about the case of Anna O. and the issue of Freud's abandonment of the seduction theory. I deal with those of Freud's basic scientific ideas that, from the perspective of contemporary biology and neuroscience, are either wrong or highly questionable. I also indicate in several places differences between Freud's original views and those of contemporary psychoanalysts. I do not, however, try to present contemporary psychoanalysis fully. My focus remains on introducing Freud.

I make no claim to completeness either in the presentation of Freud's ideas or in my brief and partial critique of some of them. I focus only on essential works. Others from Freud's massive output I mention only briefly, sometimes only as titles, and many I do not mention at all. Even with the essential works, I do not in any case deal with every ramification or qualification of Freud's argument. I am particularly aware of the brevity of my treatment of the major case histories, each of which could be (and has been) the subject of a book-length study and of much controversy. And, given the complexity of Freud's major theoretical works from 1914 to 1926, my discussion of these works is limited to presenting the central ideas in concise form rather than elaborating on the nuances, uncertainties, and sometimes baffling contradictions of Freud's presentation. I do, however, include some basic introductory material on every aspect of Freud's wide-ranging interests—dreams, parapraxes, jokes, sexuality, neuroses, therapeutic technique, social and cultural theory, and the theory of the mind.

In his postscript to *An Autobiographical Study,* Freud says that this work "shows how psycho-analysis came to be the whole content of my life and rightly assumes that no personal experiences of mine are of any interest in comparison to my relations with that science." I have organized the chapters of this book around that statement. In chapter 1 I look at Freud's life from birth until 1886, when he begins the clinical practice that will eventually develop into psychoanalysis. After 1886 I treat his personal and professional life as one and the same. I have divided chapters 2 through 5 into chronological units in which there is a general thematic unity to Freud's work, but I also use publications from any period, earlier or later than the one under consideration, where they help in defining, summarizing, or clarifying what Freud is saying. I try to avoid oversimplification and overcomplexity. Some of the technical language of psychoanalysis is, I believe, arcane even to psychoanalysts, but some of it is unavoidable, even essential, in any introduction to Freud.

I wish to thank Michele Anctil for her thoughtful and careful typing of the manuscript, and her patience during the revisions.

Chronology

1856 Sigismund Schlomo Freud born 6 May in Freiberg, Moravia, to Jacob Freud and Amalia Nathanson, his third wife. Later in life Freud changes Sigismund to Sigmund.

1860 The Freud family moves to Vienna because of financial difficulties.

1873 Graduates from gymnasium at the head of his class.

1874 Enrolls in the faculty of medicine at the University of Vienna. In addition to regular university studies, he works in the physiology laboratory of Ernst Brücke and becomes committed to the vocation of research physiologist.

1881 Passes his examination in medicine and receives the M.D. degree.

1882 Meets Martha Bernays, falls in love, and they become engaged on 17 June. Gives up pure research and begins work at the General Hospital in Vienna, rotating through various services. In November, Josef Breuer first tells him about the case of Anna O.

1884 Publishes a monograph on cocaine.

1885 Appointed lecturer in neuropathology at the University of Vienna.

1886 Receives a travel grant and uses it to study with Jean-Martin Charcot in Paris (October 1885 to February 1886). In November he marries Martha after opening his own practice in Vienna in April.

1887–1892 Sees increasing numbers of neurotics in his private practice, and treats them at first with hypnosis.

1892–1895 Establishes many of the basic ideas of psychoanalysis and (in 1895) publishes *Studies on Hysteria* with Breuer.

1896–1899 Friendship and correspondence with Wilhelm Fliess. Death of Jacob (1896). Develops and then abandons the seduction theory. Begins self-analysis.

1900 Publishes *The Interpretation of Dreams.* "Dora" enters analysis.

1901 Publishes *The Psychopathology of Everyday Life.*

1902 Founds the Wednesday Psychological Society.

1905 Publishes *Jokes and Their Relation to the Unconscious, Three Essays on the Theories of Sexuality,* and the Dora case.

1907 Jung first visits Freud in Vienna.

1908 The first international congress of psychoanalysts at Salzburg. The Wednesday Psychological Society becomes the Vienna Psychoanalytical Society.

1909 Only visit to America at Clark University in Worcester, Massachusetts.

1910 Jung elected president of the International Psychoanalytic Association at the second international congress in Nürnberg. Freud publishes "Leonardo da Vinci and a Memory of His Childhood."

1914 Jung resigns as president of the International Psychoanalytic Association. Freud publishes "On Narcissism: An Introduction."

1915–1917 Writes and publishes five metapsychological essays.

1919 The International Psychoanalytic Press founded.

1920 Ernest Jones founds the *International Journal of Psycho-Analysis.*

1923 Publishes *The Ego and the Id.* First diagnosis of cancer.

1930 Publishes *Civilization and Its Discontents.* Receives the Goethe Prize from the city of Frankfurt.

1932 Publishes *New Introductory Lectures on Psycho-Analysis.*

1936 Eighty years old. The cancer recurs and requires a major operation.

1938 Hitler in Vienna. Determines finally to leave Vienna, which he does (with his wife and daughter, Anna) on 4 June. On 6 June reaches London, where he moves to his final home at 20 Maresfield Gardens in Hampstead. Publishes *Moses and Monotheism.* Begins work on *An Outline of Psycho-Analysis,* which is incomplete at his death and is published posthumously in 1940.

1939 Dies on 23 September at age 83.

Chapter One

The Early Life (1856–1886)

Sigismund Schlomo Freud was born 6 May 1856 at Freiberg (now Příbor in the Czech Republic) in Moravia. Sigismund was his German name, Schlomo his Jewish name (after his paternal grandfather). As early as 1872, he was using the signature "Sigmund," which, except for a brief period in 1874, he used for the rest of his life.[1] He never used his middle name.

Freud's father, Jacob, was 41 years old when Sigmund was born. He had been born in Tysmenitz—a small town in the then Habsburg province of Galicia. The Freud family may have lived in Cologne, moved eastward to Lithuania during the fourteenth or fifteenth century to flee persecution of the Jews, then migrated back to Galicia.[2] Tysmenitz was itself a center of both orthodox and liberal Jewish thought. It was also an important market town and commercial center, its commerce largely controlled by Jews who regularly traveled to the larger market towns of Breslau, Leipzig, and other German cities.[3]

In 1832, at the age of 16 and a half, Jacob married Sally Kanner, about whom almost nothing is known. They had two sons, Emanuel and Philipp, and two others who died in childhood. Sally died in 1852, at which time Jacob apparently married a woman named Rebekka. Nothing whatever is known of her. She presumably died shortly after the marriage. Sigmund's mother, Amalia Nathanson, was thus Jacob's third wife. She was living in Vienna when Jacob met and married her in 1855, but had been born in Brody in eastern Galicia, had lived for several years in Odessa, and then moved to Vienna with her parents as a child. At the time of the marriage to Jacob, Amalia was 20 years old, Jacob 40. Sigmund was the first child of a marriage that would produce six more children—two boys (one of whom died at age six months) and five girls—between 1856 and 1866.

Though the marriage took place in Vienna, Jacob's home was in Freiberg, and it was there that the couple settled. Jacob had left Tysmenitz in the late 1830s to travel with his maternal grandfather between Galicia and Moravia. The two men sold such products as wool, hemp, tallow, honey, and furs and bought untreated cloth to finish

(Krüll, 92). Jacob may have been attracted to the liberal Judaism in Tysmenitz even before these travels. But it was on these trips that he encountered for the first time the possibility of a life free of the intellectual and social confinement of the *shtetl.* With the abolition of all restrictions on Austrian Jews—including restrictions on freedom of movement—after the March revolution of 1848, Jacob was free to apply for permanent residence in Freiberg (which he apparently did) and to live or travel wherever else he wished within the Habsburg empire.

Yet Jacob did not completely abandon his Jewish heritage. The Freud household seems to have been a mixture of liberal and conservative attitudes. The family continued, for example, to observe Passover and Purim. In spite of Freud's statement about his un-Jewish education, Jacob did see to it that his eldest son read the Bible and knew some Jewish history and religion. Indeed, Jacob himself introduced young Sigmund to the Bible in Ludwig Philippson's bilingual (parallel Hebrew and German) illustrated edition. Sigmund may even have been taught some Hebrew.[4] But he was apparently never pushed by either parent to be a practicing Jew. "I was always an unbeliever" and "have been brought up without religion," he would later write.[5]

Yet, though alienated from Judaism as a religion, Freud always insists that he has "never lost the feeling of solidarity" with the Jewish people (*Letters,* 365). In his own mind, his Jewish identity is never in question, and he repeatedly acknowledges it publicly. Though not religious, and certainly not political, he tells his B'Nai B'Brith Lodge brothers, there remains "enough to make the attraction of Judaism and the Jews irresistible, many dark emotional powers all the stronger the less they could be expressed in words, as well as the clear consciousness of an inner identity." To this inexpressible inner identity, moreover, Freud attributes two indispensable qualities—freedom from prejudices that restrict the intellect and a preparedness "to be in the opposition and to renounce agreement with the 'compact majority' " (*Letters,* 367).[6] For Freud, then, his Jewishness is the basis of his most valued character traits—his intellectual independence and his defiance of social convention.

From Freiberg to Vienna

For the first four years of his life, Freud lived in Freiberg. He would always look back on these years as an almost idyllic time. As Freud's son Martin suggests, this idealized view of the Freiberg years may reflect the shock of moving to an overcrowded Jewish quarter of Vienna from the rural openness of Freiberg.[7] In "Screen Memories" (1899), speaking as a patient who is, in fact, himself, he says that he was never really comfortable in the town (that is, Vienna) to which his family was forced to move from his boyhood home. " 'I believe now,' " he continues, " 'that I was never free from a longing for the beautiful woods near our home, in which . . . I used to run off from my father, almost before I had learned to walk' " (*SE,* 3:312–13).

Yet Freiberg was not all rural idyll. The Freud family lived in a small rented room on the second floor in the house of a blacksmith. Jacob apparently made an adequate but not spectacular living as a wool merchant. But by 1860, either through his own personal failings, a general economic decline in the textile industry, or some combination of both, he was forced to move to a larger town. Even before Vienna, the Freud family was never really secure financially.[8]

Though never a successful businessman, Jacob was a good father. He was amiable, generous, and, in spite of his unsuccessful business ventures, optimistic—always "full of projects, still hoping," as Freud wrote in a letter to his fiancée (*Letters,* 86). Jacob also had a passion for learning, which he passed on to his eldest son. He recognized his son's special intellectual gifts and made it a point to tutor him, which he did until Sigmund entered the gymnasium at age nine (one year earlier than normal). Writing after Jacob's death in October 1896 at age 81, Freud says, "I valued him highly, understood him very well, and with his peculiar mixture of deep wisdom and fantastic light-heartedness he had a significant effect on my life."[9] So significant, indeed, that his father's death was a major factor, perhaps the sole factor, leading to Freud's self-analysis in the late 1890s.

Of course, this self-analysis would teach Freud that his feelings about his father were more complicated than his conscious veneration. Those conscious feelings, he discovered, were mixed with equally powerful but unconscious feelings of hostility. Yet, as Peter Gay observes, many of Freud's equivocal feelings about his father were very close to the surface.[10] Discussing his schoolboy identification with Hannibal and his war against Rome (for him, a conflict between the "tenacity of Jewry" and the Catholic Church), Freud remembers his father's story of how, as a young man, a Gentile knocked his cap off his head and into the mud, and yelled at him to get off the pavement. In answer to Freud's question as to what he did, Jacob replied that he went into the road and picked up his cap. "This struck me," Freud comments, "as unheroic conduct on the part of the big, strong man who was holding the little boy by the hand" (*SE,* 4:196–97). Freud, like Hannibal, would be defiant about his Jewishness, not pathetic and acquiescent like his father.

Perhaps Freud's passionate defiance came from his mother. Almost all students of Freud's life have commented on her eldest son's lifelong attachment to and idealization of Amalia. They have equally noted that Sigmund remained her favorite among her seven surviving children and that, from the moment of his birth in caul, she believed that he was destined to be a great man.[11] Her grandson, Martin, describes her as very emotional, as having "great vitality and much impatience; she had a hunger for life and an indomitable spirit."[12] She was always proud of the role of Jewish students (including two of her own brothers) in the 1848 revolution. Peter Newton argues that Amalia, frustrated by the circumstances of her life with Jacob, bequeathed to Sigmund her own passionate hopes and aspirations.[13] This is plausible but speculative, given the paucity of details about Amalia as a young and middle-aged woman.

On one matter Jacob and Amalia, however different in temperament, agreed—that Sigmund was exceptional and that his future greatness should be encouraged in every way possible. As one sign of his special position, Sigmund was the only member of the family to have the use of his own room for privacy and study. He occupied this room until he moved to hospital quarters in his twenties. In a time of increased opportunity for Jews, Freud was, of course, hardly the only Jewish son to be urged to fame and fortune by ambitious parents and to aspire not only to business but to the liberal professions (law, medicine, academia, journalism) from which Jews had hitherto been excluded. In Freud's case, however, this high ambition was accompanied by a powerful intellect that was capable of success in many fields.

If Freud's ambition was fueled by his parents from his earliest years, so probably was his intellectual curiosity. For Freud was surrounded by a puzzling family situation. Jacob, after all, was twice his wife's age. And the man Freud called father was also called father by two young men who were close to his mother's age. Of these two half-brothers, Emanuel, the older, lived with his wife, Maria, nearby. The couple had two children—John, one year older than Freud (who was thus born an uncle to his older nephew), and Pauline, one year younger than Freud. The younger of his two half-brothers, Philipp, was unmarried and lived directly opposite the Freuds. Then there was the Czech Catholic nursemaid who cared for Freud before she was dismissed for stealing. The complex and ambivalent emotional reaction to these people and to his younger brother and sister born during this period would later be the essential content of his self-analysis and of many of his earliest ideas about the importance of childhood experiences in shaping the adult. But this web of relationships must have been puzzling at the time, not just later. Ernest Jones rightly observes that the complexity of Freud's family relationships "must have afforded a powerful incentive to his budding intelligence, to his curiosity and interest. From earliest days he was called upon to solve puzzling problems, and problems of the greatest import to him emotionally."[14] For a man "superbly endowed in the linguistic and the personal intelligences—comfortable and competent in dealing in the realm of words and the realm of human beings," Freud's early experience of problematic relationships and feelings was a natural place to begin to use this intelligence.[15]

The move from Freiberg meant the end of this family situation. Emanuel and Philipp moved to Manchester, England. Jacob took his family first to Leipzig (for reasons unknown), and then to Vienna in 1860. They settled in the Leopoldstadt—a district of Vienna (though not incorporated until 1861) separated from the Inner City of Vienna by the Danube Canal. Many of the ethnic groups coming to Vienna in the mid-nineteenth century settled here first (and sometimes for good). Many of the Jews who later moved across the canal lived first in the Leopoldstadt.

Like many poor Jewish families with few possessions, the Freud family moved a half dozen times in 15 years. Whatever living Jacob made (and it is not clear just how he did make a living), it was not enough to get his family out of the slums that made up the center of this district. No wonder Freud would look back nostalgically to his Freiberg years.[16]

In spite of the poverty of these early years in Vienna, Freud was in many respects fortunate. For one thing, he did have a private room in a space that allowed no one else any privacy at all. For another, he was encouraged from the beginning to develop his intellectual gifts and thus, like many other Jews, to develop the means to take advantage of the opportunities in business or the professions available in Vienna. Finally, he was a young man in Vienna at just the right time. Twenty years earlier, the Freud family might not even have been able to move there. Twenty years later, and Freud's career might have been adversely affected by the increasingly organized anti-Semitism of late-nineteenth-century Vienna. From 1860 to about 1880, Freud enjoyed that brief window of time when a liberal government, as Decker observes, championed "constitutional government, a centralized state, economic freedom, full religious toleration, and secular authority over education and marriage." Assimilated, German-speaking Jews (like the Freuds), sharing the liberals' agenda, were happy to support the new government (Decker, 25).[17] In turn, they could expect to advance economically and to participate politically. As Freud later recalled, this was a time when "every industrious Jewish schoolboy carried a Cabinet Minister's portfolio in his satchel" (*SE,* 4:193).

Freud took every advantage of this situation. For most of the years at the gymnasium, he was at the head of his class. As he says in *An Autobiographical Study,* "I was at the top of my class for seven years; I enjoyed special privileges there, and had scarcely ever to be examined in class" (*SE,* 20:8). In July 1873 he passed his *Matura* examination with distinction. Interestingly, one of his assignments for this examination was the translation of a passage from Sophocles' *Oedipus Rex.* In addition to his assigned schoolwork, he also read widely in German, English, French, and Spanish literature (the last three he read in the original language, not in German translation), and he continued to be a voracious reader for the rest of his life. He read the Greek and Roman classics in the original language. He read archeology, anthropology, art history, and probably more philosophy than he cared to admit. He was a humanist physician of a kind that was not uncommon in the nineteenth century but that is hard to find now.

The Medical School Years

Freud enrolled in the medical faculty at the University of Vienna in the fall of 1873. He received his M.D. degree in 1881—three years longer than the usual five years. There are two puzzles here: first, why he chose medicine rather than the law to which he was drawn; and second, why he took so much longer than the average time to finish.

In *An Autobiographical Study,* Freud writes of his attraction to law and social activism as the result of the influence of an older schoolfriend who became a well-known politician. But he also writes of his attraction to Darwin's theories, and then observes that it was hearing a reading of Goethe's essay "On Nature" that decided him to become a medical student (*SE,* 20:8).[18] Peter Gay is rightly suspicious of this lecture as leading to a sudden and dramatic turning point in Freud's life. It must, he says, be the "final impulsion to a decision that had been ripening in Freud's mind for some time" (Gay 1988, 24).

What makes the choice of medicine even more curious is Freud's comment in *An Autobiographical Study* that neither then nor later in his life did he "feel any particular predilection for the career of a doctor" (*SE,* 20:8). But that is not just an attitude Freud took late in life. In 1896 Freud had written that "as a young man I knew no longing other than for philosophical knowledge, and now I am about to fulfill it as I move from medicine to psychology. I became a therapist against my will" (*Freud-Fliess,* 180). But if being a therapist did not attract Freud to medicine, knowledge did. He was moved, he says, "by a sort of curiosity, which was, however, directed more towards human concerns than towards natural objects" (*SE,* 20:8). Given the excitement in the late nineteenth century caused by Darwin's ideas and the growing sense that biology and medical science were entering an era of almost unimaginable new discoveries (including discoveries about man's place in nature), it is not surprising that an intellectually curious—indeed, intellectually insatiable—man like Freud would be drawn to the idea of becoming a natural scientist. Nor is it insignificant that medicine was one of the professions open to Jews.

Gay translates "by a sort of curiosity" as "a sort of greed for knowledge" (Gay 1988, 25). This translation conveys very accurately the voraciousness of Freud's university studies. In his first semester, Freud signed up for 12 lectures in anatomy and 6 in chemistry. In his second semester, he took anatomy, botany, chemistry, microscopy, and mineralogy plus, in a "characteristic overflow of interest" (Jones 1953, 1:36), a course on "Biology and Darwinism" given by Carl Claus (1835–1899) and a course on "The Physiology of the Voice and Speech" given by Ernst Brücke (1819–1892). For his third semester, he continued with anatomy, physics, phonology, and zoology for medical students. In this semester he added Franz Brentano's (1838–1917) seminar in philosophy. Finally, in the fourth semester, he attended lectures on zoology proper (rather than zoology for medical students), physiology, and physics and continued to study philosophy with Brentano. By his fifth semester, he was spending most of his time in Claus's Institute of Zoology and Comparative Anatomy and also working in Brücke's physiology laboratory. The trend is clear: Freud is moving away from the goal of becoming a medical practitioner and toward the goal of becoming a research biologist.[19]

Given this growing commitment to scientific research, and in view of Freud's later negative attitude to philosophy, Brentano seems an odd choice. Not only did he take many of Brentano's courses, he also knew him personally, visited him at his home, and even asked Brentano's advice about the feasibility of taking a doctorate in philosophy as well as in medicine (*Freud-Silberstein,* 102–5). An ex-priest, Brentano was a theist who nevertheless respected Darwin and wanted to establish psychology on an empirical basis. In 1874 he became a professor of philosophy at the University of Vienna and published his *Psychology from an Empirical Standpoint.* Freud entered his first course with Brentano in that same year.

Was this an important experience for Freud, or only a passing phase? Owen J. Flanagan and William J. McGrath argue for the former. For Flanagan, the influence on Freud of Brentano's views on intentionality is clear. Intentionality, he says, is for Brentano the "ineliminable mark of the mental." This position implies that "no language that lacks the conceptual resources to capture the meaningful content of mental states, such as the language of physics or neuroscience, can ever adequately capture the salient facts about psychological phenomena." Freud's vocabulary of conscious and unconscious belief, memory, desire, and wish provides "a framework in which intentional content figures essentially."[20] McGrath, whose argument for Brentano's influence is lengthy and detailed, says Brentano's dualistic position—that is, his assertion that the data of consciousness are divided into the class of the physical and the class of the mental and that the proper study of psychology is the properties and laws of the soul, which can only be studied by "inner perception"—offered a "highly congenial framework, a framework within which Freud was later to make his own revolutionary discoveries" (McGrath, 114). It may well be that, during the 1890s when Freud found himself having to abandon a neurophysiological for a psychological vocabulary, Brentano's teachings not only influenced his thinking about intentional phenomena but also gave him some intellectual support in moving beyond hard science. If this is so, Freud makes no reference to Brentano or his ideas. Still, it is likely that Brentano's influence was substantial in pointing Freud toward the legitimacy of studying meaning, sense, and intention in such phenomena as dreams, parapraxes (Freudian slips), and jokes. Brentano's appeal may also suggest something more. Jones reports that, in reply to Jones's question as to how much philosophy Freud had read, Freud's answer was " 'Very little. As a young man I felt a strong attraction towards speculation and ruthlessly checked it' " (Jones 1953, 1:29). This may well be true, for a speculative bent certainly emerges in some of Freud's later works. Maybe he allowed it a brief expression in his studies with Brentano.

In addition to the attraction to Brentano, another theme that seems to contradict Freud's move toward research enters the picture. Returning from a trip to England in the summer of 1875 to visit his half-brothers in Manchester, Freud wrote to his friend Eduard Silberstein that he now had "more than one ideal, a practical one having been added to the theoretical one of earlier years." Now he wants, not a laboratory and free time, but a "large hospital and plenty of money in order to reduce or wipe out some of the ills that afflict our body" (*Freud-Silberstein,* 127). Evidently the practical English had inspired his own practicality. Peter Newton argues that this letter signifies a profound and permanent shift toward the clinical. For Newton, Freud is not a reluctant healer, but a man whose wish to help human suffering is at least equal to his research ambitions. Indeed, for Newton much of Freud's intellectual conflict from 1882 to the 1890s is a conflict between these two warring commitments, and Freud's fusion of research and healing in psychoanalysis is one of his greatest personal and intellectual triumphs (Newton, 71–72). Newton thus opposes the traditional view that Freud reluctantly trained as a clinician only because a research position was not open and he needed to be able to support a wife and family.

Serious or not in this letter, Freud did not accelerate his progress toward his M.D. on his return from England. Instead, he spent most of his time in advanced zoology as a student in Carl Claus's Institute of Zoology and Comparative Anatomy. At that time, Claus was a major spokesman for Darwin's ideas in Germany—a man, indeed, who had actually met Darwin. He had been brought to Vienna to upgrade the zoology department at the university, for which purpose he selected outstanding students to work on various scientific problems. Freud was one of these students. In March 1876 Claus assigned Freud a research project that took him to the university's zoological station in Trieste. The problem: confirm or refute the claim of a Polish scientist that he had observed testes in eels and hence that eels were not hermaphrodites. Freud did confirm this claim, though inconclusively. Nevertheless, Claus sponsored this research for publication, and Freud's first scientific essay—"Observations on the Form and Finer Structure of the Lobed Organs of the Eel, Described as Testes"—appeared in 1877. On a more psychoanalytic note, it may be, as Lucille Ritvo suggests, that Freud's tendency to think in terms of development as a gradual and continuous process was one of the important ideas he took from Claus's presentation of Darwin's theory (Ritvo, 129).[21]

But Freud did not continue to work with Claus, nor does he even refer to him in *An Autobiographical Study.* It was in Brücke's physiological laboratory, he says, that "I found rest and full satisfaction—and men, too, whom I could respect and take as my models: the great Brücke himself, and his assistants, Sigmund Exner and Ernst Fleischl von Marxow" (*SE,* 20:9). Many years later Freud would refer to Brücke as the man "who carried more weight with me than any one else in my whole life" (253). The relationship with Brücke was critical for Freud's socialization as a scientist. What Brücke gave Freud, as Gay observes, "was the ideal of professional self-discipline in action" (Gay 1988, 34). He would study with Brücke until 1882, eventually becoming his laboratory assistant. It was Brücke who would advise him to abandon his research career and go into private practice. It was Brücke's influence that helped him gain the title of *Privatdozent* (something like a lecturer in an American university). And it was Brücke who helped him receive the traveling grant to Paris, where he first encountered the ideas of Jean-Martin Charcot (1825–1893) on hysteria.

Brücke's scientific ideas also made an indelible impression on Freud. A renowned physiologist, Brücke was a thoroughgoing materialist. In 1842 he and Emil Du Bois-Reymond (1818–1896) pledged to study living organisms only in terms of physical-chemical forces active in the organism. Their goal was the elimination of all traces of vitalism in biology (as represented, for example, by their own teacher, Johannes Müller).[22] In cases where physical-chemical forces do not supply an explanation, they argued, the investigator must either find a way to explain them by the physical mathematical method or " 'assume new forces equal in dignity to the chemical-physical forces inherent in matter, reducible to the force of attraction and repulsion.' "[23] Joined by Hermann Helmholtz (1821–1894) and Carl Ludwig (1816–1895), in 1845 the four men formed the Berlin Society for Physical Physiology. In 1847 Helmholtz (much admired by Freud) delivered a paper on the application to physiology of the principle of the conservation of energy and argued for the ultimate goal of reducing physiology to the laws of chemistry and physics. Though this goal was not achieved by any member of this group, it did lead to an experimental physiology that used the methods of physics and chemistry. It was to teach this experimental physiology that Brücke was appointed to the medical faculty of the University of Vienna.[24]

From Brücke, then, Freud received a materialist view of science that he never abandoned. As Jones observes, the "principles on which he constructed his theories were those he had acquired as a medical student under Brücke's influence." Emancipation from this influence did not consist in renouncing these principles but "in becoming able to apply them empirically to mental phenomena while dispensing with any anatomical basis" (Jones 1953, 1:45). In addition to a general philosophy of science, Freud also learned from Brücke the importance of exact observation. Finally, he acquired at least two basic ideas from Brücke and other sources (including Theodor Meynert, Sigmund Exner, and Gustav Fechner) that remain central to his developing theory to the end of his life: that physiological and psychological processes can be described in terms of quantities of excitation (energy) transmitted through the nervous system and that the brain functions as a unit in a reflex arc by receiving and discharging these sums of excitation. Actually, these two ideas are aspects of a single idea. The nervous system attempts to keep what Freud calls its sum of excitation constant by discharging all accretions of excitation (*SE,* 1:153–54). Erich Fromm calls this the principle of tension reduction (Freud would eventually call it the principle of constancy) and rightly sees it as an axiom "deeply fixed" in Freud's mind.[25] Brücke described the energies of mental processes interchangeably in physiological and psychological terms. Freud would later concentrate on psychic energy and on the drives that generate that energy.[26] And though, as Jones says, Freud's views imply no anatomical or neurological basis, the idea of tension reduction remains true for him in the psychic as well as in the neurological arena. This drive/discharge or tension reduction model has many ramifications in Freud's thought and in the history of psychoanalysis. For assent to or denial of drive theory is one of the intellectual reasons (possibly the major one) for the division early in the history of psychoanalysis between Freudians and neo-Freudians (sometimes called interpersonal theorists).[27] Even today many psychoanalysts distinguish between a drive and a relational paradigm.[28]

The Reluctant Clinician

Freud earned his M.D. in 1881. Even then, however, he made no attempt to obtain clinical training. Instead, he remained an assistant in Brücke's laboratory for another year and continued to publish scientific papers. He decided to leave only when Brücke urged him to abandon research and prepare for a medical career so as to make a living. Given the average of five years for receiving the M.D., Freud was now (since medical students then received no experience on hospital wards) a good four years behind the clinical experience of his classmates who had graduated on time.

Making a living was now especially important. In April 1882 Freud had met and fallen in love with 20-year-old Martha Bernays from

Wandsbek, just outside Hamburg in north Germany. Her family was religiously orthodox, highly cultured, and included a successful merchant father (who had died in 1879), scholarly uncles, and a grandfather who had been the chief rabbi of Hamburg. Though Freud was too poor to marry, the couple became secretly engaged only two months after meeting. For most of the next four years, Martha lived in Wandsbek, Freud in Vienna. This period is recorded in the numerous letters that Freud wrote to Martha.[29]

In July 1882 Freud began to train at the General Hospital of Vienna. He spent three years (1882–1885) rotating through a number of medical specialties including surgery (very briefly), internal medicine, psychiatry, dermatology, nervous diseases (organic), and ophthalmology. He worked for five months in the psychiatric clinic of Theodor Meynert (1833–1892), who had greatly impressed him as a student and whom he thought (as did many others) was the greatest brain anatomist of his day. This was his only training in psychiatry. Those who continue to think of Freud as the father of modern psychiatry are entirely misinformed. He was a neurologist who was the father of psychoanalysis, which in the twentieth century has maintained at best an uneasy alliance with psychiatry. More often than not, the two have gone entirely separate ways.

Meynert was uninterested in therapy but greatly interested in brain anatomy, so Freud found himself once again doing research. He clearly worked very hard during these years, was proud of his ability to be in full charge of many patients, and, on the basis of his hospital work and clinical publications, was appointed *Privatdozent* in 1885. He debated general practice as against specialization, but, as a letter of 29 August 1888 shows, he realized that he had not learned enough medicine to be a general practitioner. He had, he says, been "able to learn just about enough to become a neuropathologist" (*Freud-Fliess,* 23).

Neuropathologist here means neurologist—a field for which he had some qualification from his years of study of neuroanatomy and neurophysiology and that was if anything underrepresented in Vienna. Freud thus had both a practical and a theoretical reason for being drawn to this subject. At that time, to think of neurology was to think of Charcot, with whom Freud accordingly determined to study. For this purpose, he applied for and, in October 1885, received a travel grant to study in Paris with Charcot.

So far, Freud had succeeded admirably in his work as a student and as a doctor in training. But he did have one setback to his reputation. This came as a result of his experiments with and advocacy of cocaine.

Intending, as he told Martha, to study its effects in cures of heart trouble and nervous exhaustion, he was soon taking it himself and recommending it to all of his friends. Anxious for a shortcut to fame and money, he also rushed into print in 1884 with an article entitled "On Coca" in which he extolled the many therapeutic virtues of cocaine. The only good thing to come of this hasty publication was Carl Koller's (1857–1944) follow-up on Freud's suggestion of the numbing effect of cocaine on the lips and tongue by using it as an anesthetic in eye surgery. Koller thus received credit for the invention of local anesthesia. But Freud's attempt to wean Fleischl von Marxow from morphine addiction by recommending cocaine ended disastrously with his friend becoming addicted to cocaine. Moreover, as Jones observes, with cocaine addiction being reported from around the world, Freud's reputation suffered (Jones 1953, 1:94).[30] This would not be the last time Freud rushed into print.

Charcot

Freud arrived in Paris in October 1885 and left at the end of February 1886. These were a decisive four months. Indeed, this period, like the much longer medical school period, was a turning point in Freud's life. He went to Paris to study a problem in neuroanatomy—an indication of continuing preference for research over clinical activities. He left, as he says in his "Report on My Studies in Paris and Berlin" (*SE*, 1:5–15), with a lively interest in hysteria and hypnosis. As much as anything else, this transformation was effected by the warmth, kindness, and brilliance of Charcot.

In 1885 Charcot had been working on hysteria for a number of years and was just beginning to experiment with hypnosis. Behind him lay a distinguished career as a neurologist in the Salpêtrière—the old saltpeter depot that had been converted into a hospital for women. Arriving there in the 1850s, he had found five thousand women lying in poorly lit wards. Moving through the wards, he began to sort out the different pathologies and, in particular, to describe and name the neurological diseases present in many of the patients. This identification of disease syndromes required hours of patient observing of individual women, of looking long and carefully (as William Osler would later teach doctors to do), and of gradually sorting symptoms into discrete disease entities (such as multiple sclerosis and amyotrophic lateral sclerosis).[31] Freud noted and was attracted by this careful clinical observation and careful grouping of symptoms, as he says in his obituary on Charcot in 1893 (*SE,* 3:12–13).

The simple fact that Charcot studied hysteria, Freud says, restored dignity to a disease that many assumed to be simply a case of malingering. But what Charcot found was equally important. Discovering that in hysteria he could not locate a lesion in the central nervous system (as he could, say, with multiple sclerosis), Charcot fell back on careful clinical description. As Freud observes, "he gave a complete description of its phenomena, demonstrated that these had their own laws and uniformities, and showed how to recognize the symptoms which enable a diagnosis of hysteria to be made" (20). In addition to his description of the four-part hysterical seizure, Charcot also carefully delineated the so-called stigmata (symptoms present between the seizures)—paralysis, anesthesia, difficulty in walking and standing, tunnel vision, and hysterogenic points on the body (points that, if pressed, either started or stopped a seizure). He also described male as well as female hysteria (though he was not the only one to do so) and contributed to the death of the old idea that hysteria was connected with the uterus (in Greek, *hystera*) and hence that only women could have hysteria. For Charcot hysteria was a disease not of the uterus but of the central nervous system.

In at least two respects Charcot came close to a psychological explanation for hysteria. First, he was able to induce or (briefly) eliminate hysterical symptoms with hypnosis. Second, in his study of traumatic hysteria—neurosis secondary to fright or shock—he came close to understanding ideas as the source of the symptoms. As one of his patients who had developed a weakness on his right side and anesthesia after being frightened by a clap of thunder told him, this experience " 'gave me the idea that I could be hit by lightning' " (Drinka, 115). Freud, of course, would later give the idea as a purely psychological matter priority over any other cause of the symptom. Yet Charcot, in spite of the absence of a physical lesion at autopsy, never gave up the idea of a physical cause for hysteria. Nor did he ever abandon the idea of hereditary degeneracy as the ultimate basis of hysteria. He posited a lesion, though not one that could be observed at autopsy, which he called "functional"—a lesion of the nervous system so general and non-specific that it could not be observed. In his 1893 paper "Some Points for a Comparative Study of Organic and Hysterical Motor Paralysis," Freud explicitly rejects this definition of functional. Even a functional lesion caused by edema, he argues, would necessarily share the "characteristics of organic paralyses." That is, functional paralysis of a physical kind must, like all organic paralysis, obey the laws of the distribution of the nerves. Hysterical paralysis and other symptoms of hysteria behave "*as though anatomy did not exist or as though it had no knowledge of it*" (*SE,* 1:168–69; Freud's italics). For example, anesthesia of the hand with no anesthesia in parts of the arm is anatomically impossible, but can occur in hysteria. By 1896 in "Heredity and Aetiology of the Neuroses," Freud fully rejects Charcot's idea that a hereditary nervous disposition alone causes hysteria. It is true that Charcot directed Freud's interests to hysteria and hypnosis. But he did not determine Freud's conclusions on either subject.

On hypnosis Charcot was as thorough in his observations as with hysteria. In 1882 he presented a paper outlining three stages of hypnosis—catalepsy, lethargy, and somnambulism. As a result of his examination of the mental and physical phenomena of hypnosis, he concluded that hypnosis was an artificial neurosis and that hypnotizability was a sign of hysteria.

Charcot's views were challenged by Hippolyte Bernheim (1840–1919), a professor of internal medicine at the University of Nancy. In 1884 he questioned the reality of Charcot's three stages of hypnosis and argued that these stages occurred because of suggestion. The hypnotized patients simply fulfilled Charcot's expectations. Bernheim also insisted that many adults and most children can be hypnotized, not just hysterics. He used hypnotic suggestion to cure a variety of diseases, which means that under hypnosis the patient is told that on awakening the symptoms being treated will be gone.[32]

In the battle between Charcot and Bernheim that followed Bernheim's paper, Freud, as Gay nicely says, "vacillated" (Gay 1988, 51). He translated both Charcot and Bernheim into German and even visited Bernheim in 1889 to improve his hypnotic technique. In his "Preface to the Translation of Bernheim's *Suggestion*" (1889), Freud presents Bernheim's belief in the medical value of hypnotism enthusiastically. Yet he expresses his reservation about suggestion by the physician as an adequate explanation for it. What is at stake is the objectivity of the symptoms of hysteria, which, so he argues, are not peculiar to Charcot's patients but are the same in all times and places (*SE,* 1:75–85). Freud would later put the matter very succinctly. He might, he says, have called up the state in which a patient has access to all of his or her psychical experiences, but he did not create that state "since its features—which are, incidentally, found universally—came as such a surprise to me" (*SE,* 2:101). These issues regarding hypnosis were of interest to

Freud only as long as he relied on it as a therapeutic method. But the problem of suggestion continued to bother Freud to the end of his life, as did the issue of whose construction is the reality of the analytic situation.[33]

Return to Vienna

Freud left Paris in February 1886. He went first to Berlin, where he studied children's paralysis. He needed to learn something about this subject in order to take a position as director of the neurological department of the public Institute for Children's Diseases. Max Kassowitz (1842–1913), a pediatrician friend of his, had offered him this position before he left for Paris. Freud worked at the institute several times a week for many years, and while there wrote nine papers, all of them on children's paralysis (Jones 1953, 1:212, 216–19). The German neurologist Paul Vogel, who was until his illness and death preparing a critical edition of Freud's preanalytic writings that would include these neurological papers, has suggested on the strength of these papers that Freud should be viewed as the father of neuropediatrics.[34] Whether that is true or not, this aspect of Freud's professional activity is too often overlooked. In fact, he continued to publish on neurological subjects until almost the end of the 1890s. His first book, *On Aphasia* (1891), is often considered his most important contribution to neurology, and by some as a work that contains many psychoanalytic ideas. His last neurological work, *Infantile Cerebral Paralysis,* appeared in 1897.

On his return to Vienna, Freud continued to work in Meynert's laboratory and between May 1885 and August 1886 published three papers on neuroanatomy (his last on this subject). He also opened a practice. Finally, after four long years, he and Martha married on 13 September 1886. Within a year, their first child (Mathilde) was born. Five other children were born between 1887 and 1895—three boys and two girls. In 1891, the Freuds moved both residence and professional office to Berggasse 19, where they remained until 1938 and the coming of the Nazis.

One final event in 1886 deserves mention. In October Freud gave a lecture (as required by his travel fellowship) to the professors of the faculty of medicine. The title was "On Male Hysteria," in which he reported on what he had learned from Charcot. Rightly or wrongly, Freud felt that he received a bad reception to this lecture (though the report of the discussion does not support this interpretation). Freud probably expected much more praise than he should realistically have hoped for. In any case, the episode begins a period of Freud's life when he feels totally isolated from the medical community in which he had so long lived. Viewing the event developmentally, Newton observes that Freud, approaching the age-30 transition, was ready to strike out on his own and that he no longer needed or wanted the help of these older men (of whom Meynert was one) (Newton, 131). Freud was, or felt he was, challenged by Meynert to produce a case of male hysteria—though, since at least two of the discussants said that male hysteria was well known, it is not clear why he should have been so challenged. Nevertheless, six weeks later Freud presented "Observation of a Severe Case of Hemi-Anaesthesia in a Hysterical Male" (*SE,* 1:25–31). Though there was some applause this time, Freud persisted in thinking himself rejected. For a man who was newly married and going into private practice, Freud was not very diplomatic in offending his medical colleagues and letting them know that he was angry. Sometimes his defiance of the compact majority could backfire. And, indeed, Freud's early years in practice were very precarious financially.

Chapter Two

Becoming a Psychoanalyst (1887–1899)

In *Extraordinary Minds,* Howard Gardner says that Freud is "energized by three motivations: pleasure in classifying, lust for problem solving, passion for system building."[1] I assume that Gardner means intellectually energized, for Freud was certainly energized by other things—ambition, for example. As a formula for Freud's intellectual motivation, then, these three passions do seem to cover the full range of his activities. In this chapter I examine each of these activities in the period from 1887 to 1899—often referred to as Freud's preanalytic period.

The Classifier

Freud admired Charcot as a nosologist of neurological diseases. In his attempt to bring clinical order to neurosis, Freud became a nosologist of the neuroses. Of course, as a neurologist he saw other than neurotic patients. For example, he treated Philip Bauer (father of Ida, whom Freud calls Dora) for tertiary syphilis. So he may have seen other, more strictly organic cases in his private practice. If so, there is no record of them in the many letters he wrote to his friend Wilhelm Fliess (1858–1928) from 1887 to 1904. Rather, in these letters Freud is fully concerned with the neuroses. This is not surprising. Freud had, after all, returned from Paris with high interest in hysteria. Also, as Jones observes, like all neurologists "he found that his practice would consist largely of psychoneurotics who were under the impression that 'nerve specialists' could cure 'nerves' as well as diseases of the spinal cord" (Jones 1953, 1:228–29). So it was natural that, given Freud's intellectual interest in hysteria and his medical specialty, he would have many nervous patients in his practice.

In addition to hysteria, one other nervous disorder had recently been named—neurasthenia, which means a state of nervous weakness or exhaustion. The father of neurasthenia was an American physician named George Miller Beard (1839–1883) of New York. For Beard (whose work Freud knew well) neurasthenia could include almost any of a long list of symptoms from weakness and fatigue to various skin, gastrointestinal, cardiac, and other signs (Drinka, 189).[2] The nervous weakness causing these symptoms resulted from either a proper or improper use of a person's available nerve energy or from an oversensitive person's response to the hectic pace of modern life.[3] Beard thought that neurasthenia was peculiarly a disease of the modern world—especially in America, where the most progressive people on earth were "most prone to nervous irritability and therefore more susceptible to nervous exhaustion" (Drinka, 192). Neurologists in America and Europe agreed, and neurasthenia became a very popular diagnosis. Therapy included such things as bed rest, hydrotherapy, electrical stimulation, the rest cure and dieting advocated by S. Weir Mitchell (1829–1914), and hypnosis. Freud knew and used most of these techniques.[4]

It is surprising to learn how much time Freud gives to the diagnosis, treatment, and theory of neurasthenia. But he does. In many of the drafts he sent to Fliess (drafts A, B, and E), he addressed the issue of the cause and treatment of neurasthenia and summarized many of the points that appear in his published work on the subject.[5] Clearly neurasthenia made up a sizable proportion of his practice.

In "Heredity and the Aetiology of the Neuroses" (1896)—in which the word "psychoanalysis" first appears—Freud summarizes his conclusions as to the classification of the major neuroses (*SE,* 3:143–56).[6] There are four: hysteria, obsessional neurosis, neurasthenia, and anxiety neurosis. Hysteria and obsessional neurosis he links together as the psychoneuroses (later, the transference neuroses), a term that replaces the earlier neuro-psychoses of defense in an essay of that title (1894).[7] He also links neurasthenia and anxiety neurosis, as he explains in "On the Grounds for Detaching a Particular Syndrome from Neurasthenia under the Description 'Anxiety Neurosis' " (1895). These neuroses are usually mixed rather than pure. A person can have both hysteria and anxiety neurosis at the same time—indeed, is most likely to have both at the same time. In addition to these four major neuroses, Freud also reports two cases of psychosis—one of hallucinatory confusion in "The Neuro-Psychoses of Defence," the other a case of chronic paranoia in "Further Remarks on the Neuro-Psychoses of Defence" (1896). But he does not attempt a classification of these two cases or of psychosis in general. As a neurologist in private practice, he rarely encountered psychosis. His patients were mostly ambulatory and generally functional in daily life except for their neurotic symptoms.

The Problem Solver

Like other doctors of his time, Freud is not only interested in classifying disease syndromes. He also wants to understand their etiology, and he wants to know how to treat them. If possible, he wants a specific etiology—something with the specificity of the tubercle bacillus without which (whatever other factors contribute to the illness) tuberculosis cannot occur. Draft D (1984) to Fliess is entitled "On the Etiology and Theory of the Major Neuroses" and shows his concern over the topic.

He begins "Heredity and the Aetiology of the Neuroses" by rejecting the prevailing etiological view that nervous heredity is the true cause of neurosis. This means disagreeing with Charcot. In fact, Freud does not abandon heredity as a cause, merely as the specific cause. There are, he says, preconditions, concurrent causes, and specific causes. Preconditions, such as heredity, are general influences and present etiologically in many disorders. They are not specific to neurosis. Concurrent causes are influences—such as emotional disturbances, physical exhaustion, acute illness, intoxications, traumatic accidents, and intellectual overwork—that can precipitate many disorders (including neurosis) but that may or may not be present in the onset of those disorders. They are, as Freud says, agents provocateurs. Only specific causes are indispensable in producing an illness.

The main concession Freud makes to heredity (and which he never fully abandons) is that heredity and the specific cause in neurosis "can replace each other as regards quantity." That is, a "severely loaded nervous heredity" may contribute to neurosis even when the specific cause is slight, or "a very serious specific aetiology" may cause neurosis even when the hereditary disposition is moderate (147). In *Three Essays on the Theory of Sexuality* (1905), in a discussion of the relationship between constitutional and accidental factors in the etiology of neurosis, he describes the relationship between heredity and specific cause (here infantile sexuality) as a complemental series in which the "diminishing intensity of one factor is balanced by the increasing intensity of the other" (*SE,* 7:239–40). There may be extreme cases at each end of this series, but for Freud most neuroses are to be found somewhere along the spectrum between the two extremes and hence represent a mixture of hereditary and accidental experiences.

The specific cause of neurosis, Freud says, lies in the sexual life of the subject. It may lie in a disorder of the subject's contemporary sexual life or past sexual life. One year earlier in *Studies on Hysteria,* Freud had discussed sexual factors in the neuroses but had not asserted that they were always present.[8] Now he is explicit about its role, as he is again two years later in "Sexuality in the Aetiology of the Neuroses" (1898). In fact, sexuality always remains central for Freud, but after 1900 it will no longer be simply the genital sexuality he is talking about in these early essays.

In neurasthenia and anxiety neurosis, the sexual problem is in the present—hence the term "actual neuroses," which he first uses in "Sexuality in the Aetiology of the Neuroses." Neurasthenia, characterized by fatigue, intracranial pressure, dyspepsia, constipation, spinal paraesthesias, and sexual weakness, is caused by excessive masturbation or spontaneous emission. It is thus an illness caused by impoverished excitation. That is, the neurasthenic has exhausted his nervous energy with inappropriate sexual activities.

Anxiety neurosis is the antithesis of neurasthenia. It is a neurosis of accumulated excitation. Behind the symptoms of anxiety neurosis, there is always a story of abstinence, unconsummated sexual excitement, imperfect or interrupted coitus, and sexual efforts that exceed the person's capacity. In each of these cases, Freud argues, there is an accumulation of sexual tension as a consequence of prevented discharge. So "anxiety neurosis is a neurosis of damming up, like hysteria, hence their similarity" (*Freud-Fliess,* draft E, 79–80). In both neurasthenia and anxiety neurosis, there is no psychic content to the symptoms, which are caused entirely by the somatic excess or deficiency of sexual excitation. Treatment of both the actual neuroses, as Freud discusses briefly in "Sexuality in the Aetiology of the Neuroses," involves a modification of the patient's contemporary sexual activity. Unfortunately, he is frustratingly silent on just how effective his recommendations for such change are (*SE,* 3:263–85).

The actual neuroses are rarely mentioned by Freud after the 1890s. In 1912 he refers to them in his contribution to a discussion on masturbation, defends his original position, and even says that, in spite of being without psychic content, the actual neuroses can benefit from analytic treatment, which facilitates a change of sexual behavior (*SE,* 12:243-54). In "On Narcissism: An Introduction" (1914), he suggests that hypochondria be regarded as a third actual neurosis (*SE,* 14:83). In *An Autobiographical Study* he admits that neither he nor anyone else has pursued a study of the actual neuroses but also says that, looking back on his findings, "they seem to me still to hold good" (*SE,* 20:26). So far as I know, the actual neuroses have been absent from psychoanalysis since the 1920s.

Yet two consequences remain as a legacy of Freud's thinking about these neuroses, one explicit, the other implicit. The first is Freud's original theory of anxiety. In developing a theory of anxiety neurosis in the 1895 essay on that topic, Freud first uses the term "libido," and he goes on to observe that many cases of anxiety neurosis involve a decrease of sexual libido or psychical desire. Evidently, he thinks of libido as psychical. Normally, he says, sexual excitation moves from the somatic to the psychical and then seeks appropriate discharge in the external world. If something intervenes (abstinence, say), the psychical libido is abnormally deployed and is transformed into anxiety. As Freud says in an abstract of this 1895 essay, which he prepared in 1897, "*Neurotic anxiety is transformed sexual libido*" (*SE,* 3:251; Freud's italics). This view of anxiety as the result of dammed-up libido persists unchanged until his last major theoretical work—*Inhibitions, Symptoms, and Anxiety* (1926).

The second consequence is equally important though somewhat ambiguously stated. Early in "Heredity and the Aetiology of the Neuroses," Freud comments on Beard's belief that neurasthenia is caused by the wear and tear of modern civilization and says that he does not accept this view. Having missed the specific etiology of neurasthenia, Beard misses two important insights. One, of course, is simply the sexual etiology of neurasthenia. The other Freud addresses in " 'Civilized' Sexual Morality and Modern Nervousness" (1908), where he observes that Beard and all others who miss this sexual etiology falsely conclude that neurasthenia is a disease of modern life. In fact, Freud says, it is a disease of civilization in all times and places since civilization creates nervousness by its demands on instinct, especially the sexual instinct (*SE,* 9:181–204). Freud here begins a theme—that civilization is built on instinctual renunciation—that recurs through many later works and culminates in *Civilization and Its Discontents* (1930).

Unlike the actual neuroses, the psychoneuroses remain central to Freud's work. I have already discussed the role of Charcot in arousing Freud's interest in hysteria. But that interest began long before Charcot. In November 1882, and again in July 1883, Josef Breuer (1842–1925) talked to Freud about an interesting case he had treated from December 1880 to June 1882—a 21-year-old woman named Bertha Pappenheim (1859–1936), whom Breuer calls "Anna O." in *Studies on Hysteria.* Fourteen years older than Freud, Breuer was one of the most successful practicing physicians in Vienna and also a man of scientific interests. Indeed, he worked in Brücke's laboratory, where he first met Freud in the late 1870s. The relationship quickly became a close one personally and intellectually. Breuer often loaned Freud money and later referred patients to the new practitioner. They remained close until personal and intellectual differences ended the friendship around the time of their joint authorship of *Studies on Hysteria.*[9]

Anna's illness began in December 1880 when she was nursing her dying father to whom she was devoted.[10] She became weak, anorexic, and anemic. Breuer was asked to see her because of a chronic cough, which he diagnosed as nervous in origin. Now in bed, Anna developed additional symptoms—a convergent squint, paralysis and anesthesia in the arms and legs, left-sided occipital headache, disturbances of vision, altered states of consciousness (one melancholy, the other agitated and often hallucinatory), and an inability to speak her native German (she could speak in English, sometimes French and Italian). In the afternoon she fell into a somnolent state that lasted until after sunset, when she fell into a deeper sleep, which she called "clouds." Breuer discovered that if, while in this cloud state, Anna told him stories she would calm down, but he had to listen to these stories (all sad) every day to get this effect. Anna referred to this treatment as "chimney-sweeping" or "the talking cure."

After the father's death in April 1881, Anna developed terrifying hallucinations, and the paralysis and anesthesia worsened. Finally, Breuer discovered a way to remove the symptoms. In the summer (probably of 1881) Anna developed an inability to drink water or any other liquid. For six weeks she lived only on fruit. One day, in her cloud state, Anna complained about an English lady companion (whom she disliked) and described how she had once been in the lady's room and seen her dog drink water out of a glass. Anna was disgusted but, wanting to be polite, said nothing. After venting her anger at this remembered scene, she asked for a drink of water, drank, awakened from her trance, and the symptom disappeared. Breuer now began to hypnotize Anna and ask her to recollect the circumstances under which each of her other symptoms had appeared. Each symptom, he found, was traceable to a traumatic event of which Anna had no memory and that disappeared when she recalled the situation and the emotion it aroused. By June 1882 all the symptoms were gone, and, Breuer concludes in *Studies on Hysteria,* she has been completely healthy since then.

But that turns out not to be true, and Breuer certainly knew it. For, as Henri Ellenberger has discovered, in July 1882 (just after Anna's supposed cure in June) Breuer and Anna's family placed her in the Bellevue Sanatorium in Kreuzlingen, Switzerland, where she remained until 29

October. In addition to symptoms of hysteria, she suffered from a serious trigeminal (facial) neuralgia, which she had had for six months, and morphine addiction.[11] According to Albrecht Hirschmüller, Anna was in another sanatorium at least three times between 1883 and 1887 (Hirschmüller, 115).

Why did Breuer falsely claim a complete cure? Was he simply lying? Or did Anna in fact get rid of all her symptoms and then something else happen to make admission to the sanatorium necessary? Here Freud enters the picture. In a letter of 2 June 1932, he claims that he guessed what that something else was after remembering a comment of Breuer's in another context. On the very evening of the day when the last symptom had disappeared, Breuer was summoned to Anna and found her in the throes of false pregnancy, believing that she was delivering Breuer's baby. Breuer then "took flight and abandoned the patient to a colleague" (*Letters,* 413). In his flight he missed the chance to understand transference and the erotic basis of hysteria, both of which Freud would go on to explore.

Like everything else about the case, Freud's story of the false pregnancy has been questioned. For Mikkel Borch-Jacobsen, it is no more than a "psychoanalytic myth based on rumor and professional gossip."[12] This may be a bit harsh, but it is true that except for Freud's guess there is no hard evidence for the episode. For Borch-Jacobsen, further, the founding myth of psychoanalysis—Anna's treatment and cure—is a total fabrication based on Breuer's inability to understand that Anna was really a compliant patient who gave her physician the symptoms she thought he wanted. The whole case, in short, was based on suggestion.[13]

Were it not for Freud's repeated habit of pointing to Breuer's case as the beginning of psychoanalysis, none of this would matter. But he does.[14] That makes the case a central one for the history of psychoanalysis and thus a major target for critics of psychoanalysis. Had Freud ever met or treated Anna, the damage would be even greater. Fortunately, he didn't, so whatever happened during her treatment was due to Breuer. Did Breuer ever really understand what happened between him and Anna? Did he give the cure a happy ending to protect himself or the method of treatment? Did Freud push Breuer to accept his own ideas on traumatic hysteria as derived from Charcot? Or was Breuer independent and knowledgeable enough to think through the theoretical implications of his treatment of Anna on his own? Borch-Jacobsen argues that he only came to think about the cause under pressure from a Freud armed with new ideas on traumatic hysteria learned from Charcot (Borch-Jacobsen, 53–61). But I'm not sure. Breuer was, after all, a scientist in his own right, capable of forming his own conclusions independently of Freud—as he did, for example, in his theoretical understanding of hysteria.

Whatever was really wrong with Anna and whatever happened between her and Breuer, this was the case Freud was interested in on his return from Paris. They discussed the case together and also reviewed Breuer's case notes. Much against his will, Breuer was finally convinced to publish the case in a book authored by both men on the theory and treatment of hysteria. In the meantime, Freud began to use hypnosis, probably in the form of hypnotic suggestion such as in the case reported in the 1892 paper "A Case of Successful Treatment by Hypnosis" (*SE,* 1:117–28). He probably started using Breuer's technique of looking for traumatic memories in patients under hypnosis in 1887 or 1888. His first patient may have been Anna von Lieben (1847–1900), the Frau Cäcilie M. of *Studies on Hysteria,* whom Freud treated until 1893 and whose case history is distributed through the book in fragments. In the first year of her treatment she went to see Charcot in Paris, and she is probably the patient who accompanied Freud on his visit to see Bernheim. Shortly after von Lieben came Fanny Moser (1848–1924), the Frau Emmy von N. of *Studies on Hysteria.*[15] With Frau Emmy he used a combination of suggestion and Breuer's cathartic technique.

The idea of the technique as cathartic first appears in "On the Psychical Mechanism of Hysterical Phenomena: Preliminary Communication," which Breuer and Freud coauthored in 1893 and which became the first chapter of *Studies on Hysteria* (*SE,* 2:3–17). Their initial argument is clear: hysterics are ruled by memories of which they are unaware. In the words of the famous formula, *"Hysterics suffer mainly from reminiscences"* (7; Breuer and Freud's italics). The symptoms of hysteria are strictly related to the trauma of this memory, proof of which, the authors claim, is that each hysterical symptom disappears when the memory of the event by which it was caused and the affect accompanying that event are brought to awareness (6).

Why should memories and their affect cause hysterical symptoms? Because, Breuer and Freud say, in cases of hysteria there has not been a normal reaction (tears, acts of revenge, even expression in language) to an event that arouses affect. The memory of this event acts like a foreign body long after the event itself. Such memories correspond to traumatic events that have not been sufficiently or appropriately abreacted—that is, discharged. A truly cathartic reaction to a traumatic event is an adequate one—to take revenge, for example. And the failure of abreaction occurs in "two sets of conditions under which the reaction to the trauma fails to occur" (10). The first condition is the psychical state of the person when the event occurs—a state that includes periods of fright, "abnormal psychical states, such as the semi-hypnotic twilight state of day-dreaming, auto-hypnoses, and so on" (11). In such states there is a tendency to disassociation or splitting of consciousness. There emerges a state of consciousness that the authors call "hypnoid" and in which emerging ideas are "very intense but are cut off from associative communication with the rest of the content of consciousness" (12). Though Breuer and Freud write as if both agree with this idea, the concept of the hypnoid state is Breuer's. In persons prone to such a state (like Anna), a traumatic event with affect produces hysteria because the hypnoid state is inaccessible to consciousness—indeed, can only be reached and brought into relation with normal consciousness through hypnosis.

The second condition is basically Freud's. In this view a trauma that excludes a reaction (because of the loss of someone loved, or due to social circumstances, or because of something the person wants to forget) is "intentionally repressed" from conscious thought (10). This is the first use of the word "repression" in something like its psychoanalytic sense, and with its use Freud introduces the idea of defense as a causative agent in hysteria. Only a year after the publication of *Studies on Hysteria,* in "The Aetiology of Hysteria" Freud abandons the concept of hypnoid states (*SE,* 3:194–95). From then on he works only with the idea of defense hysteria or, more generally, defense neuroses.[16] In *Studies on Hysteria,* however, whether the hysteria is defense or hypnoid, therapy is the same cathartic procedure. Under hypnosis the strangulated affect of the memory finds a way out through speech and is therefore subjected *"to associative correction by introducing it into normal consciousness"* (*SE,* 2:17; Breuer and Freud's italics).

Freud's earliest concept of defense centers on the idea of a splitting of consciousness, the motive for which comes from a person's refusal to come to terms with unpleasant ideas. As he says in "The Neuro-Psychoses of Defence," the essential feature of the neuro-psychoses (later the psychoneuroses) is an incompatibility of ideational life. This means, simply, that the ego (here not a technical term but simply person or agent) is faced with an idea or feeling that "aroused such a distressing affect that the subject decided to forget about it because he had no confidence in his power to resolve the contradiction between that incompatible idea and his ego by means of thought-activity" (*SE,* 3:47). It is interesting in these early essays how often Freud implies that the act of suppression is intentional in the sense of being conscious or half-conscious. Later, he clearly views repression as unconscious.

The trouble with suppressing an incompatible idea is that the ego is not powerful enough to efface both idea and affect. What the ego can do is to rob the idea of the "sum of excitation" with which it is loaded (48). The idea is now weak, but the detached sum of excitation (roughly, affect) must be put to another use. In hysteria the sum of excitation is transformed into a somatic symptom, which Freud calls (using the word for the first time) conversion. The memory trace of the repressed idea, which has not been dissolved, "forms the nucleus of a second psychical group," which means, apparently, that it is unconscious (49).[17]

With obsession the situation is different. A person who becomes neurotic, who lacks the capacity for conversion, but who is faced with the problem of suppressing an incompatible idea by separating it from its affect must leave that affect entirely in the psychical sphere. The idea is now weakened but conscious. Its affect attaches itself to other ideas, which then turn into obsessional ideas (51–52). To illustrate: A woman with obsessional self-reproaches constantly thinks herself guilty of something—counterfeiting or murder, for example. Indeed, she often confesses to these crimes. On analysis, her obsessive guilt turns out to be the result of excessive masturbation and the self-reproaches that this activity arouses and that attach themselves to other crimes (55). This is a very crude understanding of obsession compared to what Freud later achieves. Yet it is an understanding, and a purely psychological one at that. With hysteria the issue is somewhat unclear because of the somatic conversion. But obsession occurs entirely in the psychic sphere. There is no functional lesion and no hypnoid state that implies a central nervous system deficit of some kind.[18]

In spite of Freud's apparent agreement with Breuer's hypnoid state as one mechanism of producing hysteria, two of his four cases (Miss Lucy R. and Fräulein Elisabeth von R.) in their book are examples of defense hysteria. Because of its simplicity, I take the case of Miss Lucy R. as exemplary of a defense hysteria (*SE,* 2:106–24). Lucy was an English governess employed by a widower to care for his two girls. She was troubled by the smell of burnt pudding, a symptom that had begun two months before she first saw Freud. A letter had arrived from her mother in Glasgow while she was playing at cooking with the girls. The children grabbed the letter and forgot the pudding, which burned. The smell had pursued her since that time. Freud discovered that the letter had arrived at a time when she was thinking about going back to her mother's and leaving the children. She was also disturbed that the other servants in the house thought badly of her. Finally, she was conflicted about leaving because she had promised the children's dead mother (a distant relative) that she would never leave them. Lucy agreed with Freud's conclusion that she was in love with her employer and hoped to take the mother's place.

Some weeks later, Freud discovered that the smell of burnt pudding had been replaced by a smell resembling cigar smoke. Analysis of the cigar smell led to two earlier memories—one a dinner where her employer shouted at a male guest who was about to kiss his children (at the time the men were smoking cigars), the other an earlier scene where her employer had turned on Lucy when a female guest had kissed his children. And this last scene, Freud realizes, is the operative trauma, for it had occurred when Lucy thought that her employer might return her feelings and was shocked to discover that she was really only a governess to him.

There are traumatic moments and memories in this case—three of them, in fact. Yet, interestingly, Freud does not focus on them. Instead, he sees Lucy's problem as the "incompatibility" between a "single idea that is to be repressed and the dominant mass of ideas constituting the ego" (116). In Lucy's case the conflict is the incompatibility between being in love with her employer (which, as Freud says, she knows and doesn't know) and her awareness of being a governess and a poor girl in a rich household. The significant theoretical point is that neurotic conflict always involves such an incompatibility (which may often be based on sexuality) between the "ego and some idea presented to it"—an incompatibility usually precipitated by a traumatic event, such as Lucy's employer getting angry with her (122). Freud never abandons the idea that intrapsychic conflict is the essence of neurosis. He is usually portrayed as arriving at a purely psychological view of neurotic conflict only at the end of the 1890s. But clearly his earliest model of defense as suppressing ideas incompatible with the ego is already a purely psychological one. In only a few years, the understanding of defense against an incompatible idea is replaced by defense against an impulse and may not be as psychologically pure as the position he takes in 1894 and 1895.

In addition to defense a number of other ideas that find a permanent place in Freud's thought occur in *Studies on Hysteria.* The word "unconscious" and the idea of unconscious mental ideas first appear here—

oddly, in a section written by Breuer (*SE,* 2:222–39). Aware of the strangeness of his case histories, Freud comments on the fact that they "read like short stories" and "lack the serious stamp of science" (160). Inadvertently, it seems, he has discovered the narrative nature of memory. Finally, three important matters of technique make their first appearance in Freud's section on psychotherapy. The first is resistance, which Freud discovers when he realizes that he must overcome in his patients a psychical force that opposes making pathogenic ideas conscious. Indeed, as he presents the matter, it is the recognition of this resistance that leads him to the idea of defense, since resistance is the same force that repelled the idea in the first place (268–69). Thus the ideas of resistance and defense derive entirely from his clinical experience.

A second important technical development is free association. Unable to hypnotize many of his patients, Freud falls back on a procedure of Bernheim's. He insists to his unhypnotized patients that they will remember and continues to insist until a memory appears. To facilitate the procedure Freud has his patients lie down (on the famous couch, of course), close their eyes, and he then presses his hand to their forehead or takes their head between his hands and tells them that something will come to mind. He uses this pressure technique probably as early as Elisabeth von R. (1892) and abandons it sometime before 1900. By 1904 in "Freud's Psycho-Analytic Procedure," he says that he no longer touches his patients (*SE,* 7:249–54). He also abandons the closed eyes, though even as late as 1900 he recommends closed eyes in analysis (*SE,* 4:101). The successor to the pressure technique is free association, where the patient is urged to relax critical consciousness and communicate every idea that comes to mind on a particular subject and to omit nothing, no matter how seemingly trivial or distressing. This requirement will become the fundamental rule of psychoanalysis. Behind the conviction that free association involves meaningfully related thoughts, feelings, and ideas is Freud's belief in psychic determinism, which means that nothing mental is undetermined or random.

Finally, Freud describes transference for the first time. He notices that the patient may become frightened when "transferring on to the figure of the physician the distressing ideas which arise from the content of the analysis" (*SE,* 2:302). Though used very narrowly here, this is clearly the beginning of a central concept in Freud's work and in contemporary psychoanalysis—that in the therapeutic situation the patient repeats in the relationship with the analyst a combination of feelings, fantasies, and behaviors originally directed toward significant people in the past (especially the parents).

Sexuality also appears in *Studies on Hysteria* but, as I have indicated, not as an invariable factor. Within a year of the publication of the book, however, Freud published three essays in which he argues for a specific sexual etiology for the psychoneuroses. They are "Heredity and the Aetiology of the Neuroses," "Further Remarks on the Neuro-Psychoses of Defence," and "The Aetiology of Hysteria." Together, these essays contain Freud's account of the seduction theory of psychoneurosis—for at least the last 15 years one of the most controversial of all the controversies about Freud. The basic idea is very simple. As Freud says in "Heredity and the Aetiology of the Neuroses," traumas have occurred before puberty (usually before age 8 to 10) consisting of actual genital excitation. The abuse is committed by another person. The etiology of hysteria is a passive sexual experience to which the response is either indifference or mild fright. In obsessional neurosis the sexual event has produced pleasure (for either boy or girl) and thus leads, not to conversion, but to the self-reproaches characteristic of this neurosis (*SE,* 3:152–56). So hysterics and obsessive compulsives enter puberty with an already existing propensity for the two neuroses. Both of these neuroses, as Freud says in "Further Remarks on the Neuro-Psychoses of Defence," are "indirect consequences of sexual noxae which have occurred before the advent of sexual maturity" or, more precisely, "of the psychical memory-traces of those noxae" (*SE,* 3:168).

Puberty, then, is critical. Any postpubertal experiences that help precipitate hysteria do so only because "they arouse the memory-trace of these traumas in childhood, which do not thereupon become conscious but lead to a release of affect and to repression" (166). In short, susceptibility to hysteria exists before a postpubertal trauma. And the traumas of childhood *"operate in a deferred fashion as though they were fresh experiences; but they do so unconsciously"* (167 n; Freud's italics). In hysteria, of course, the excess excitation generated by the postpubertal trauma is converted into physical symptoms.

Again, obsession is different. Obsession begins with a pleasurable sexual experience that leads to precocious sexuality. At puberty a self-reproach is directed at these pleasurable sexual activities, which may have included the seduction of other children. The sense of pleasure is repressed and replaced by a period of conscientiousness, shame, and self-distrust that passes for health (169). There follows a failure of defense, a return of the repressed (the first use of the term), and the appearance of obsessional ideas and affects. Since repression operates in both the psychoneuroses, it is clear that the seduction theory does not eliminate the idea of defense. To the contrary, it strengthens this idea. These early traumas are not remembered consciously.

Who are the seducers? Today Freud is often vilified for hiding the role of the father as seducer—as he does, for example, in the case of Katherina in *Studies on Hysteria,* where only in 1929 does he reveal that her father, not her uncle, attempted to seduce her (*SE,* 2:134). There is no doubt that the idea of the father as seducer bothers Freud. But it is also true that, from the beginning, Freud identifies a wide array of seducers and that for him the father is never thought of as the only person to be held responsible for this act. In "The Aetiology of Hysteria," in fact, he identifies many kinds of seduction by many different people. There are random assaults by strangers. There are assaults by adults tending the child—governess, maid, tutor, and close relatives. And there are child-to-child relationships such as those between a brother and sister (*SE,* 3:208). Still, it is likely that he thought fathers more often involved than he admitted publicly.

Like the discoverer of a new microbe, Freud presents his sexual etiology of the psychoneuroses as a major medical breakthrough. In 18 cases of hysteria (6 men and 12 women), he says in "The Aetiology of Hysteria," he has discovered sexual seduction in every case and, "where the circumstances allowed, [been able] to confirm it by therapeutic success" (199).[19] Yet neither in this essay nor in the other two does he give any actual case material. So it is very difficult to know how to evaluate his own estimate of his successful discovery of the etiology and therapy of neurosis.

Then, after publishing these three essays, in a now famous letter to Fliess on 21 September 1897, he announces that he no longer believes in the seduction theory.[20] He gives four reasons for his change of mind. First, he has been unable to complete a single treatment. Some patients have even run away from therapy. Moreover, even partial success can be explained in other ways. Second, he is surprised that in all cases the father, "not excluding my own," was the seducer. The problem with this conclusion is the "unexpected frequency of hysteria," which, since not every case of seduction leads to neurosis, would mean that the incidence of perversion by the father would have to be too high to be believable. Third, he now recognizes that "there are no indications of reality in the unconscious" so that truth and fiction cannot be separated. And fourth, even in deep psychosis the "secret of childhood experiences" remains undeveloped. So it is doubtful that treatment can break through the resistance of consciousness (*Freud-Fliess,* 264–65).

In the history of psychoanalysis this letter is usually seen as a defining moment, a turning point. For, in freeing himself of the idea of a literal seduction, Freud is now able to look at these reports as fantasies. Thus, as he says in *On the History of the Psycho-Analytic Movement* (1914), a new fact emerges: the fact that patients create such fantasies means that "psychical reality requires to be taken into account alongside practical reality." The fantasies must express some constitutional need, and so behind them the "whole range of a child's sexual life came to light" (*SE,* 14:17–18). As he says to Fliess in a letter of 3 January 1899, "To the question 'What happened in earliest childhood?' the answer is, 'Nothing, but the germ of a sexual impulse existed' " (*Freud-Fliess,* 338).

But for Jeffrey Masson, Freud's abandonment of the seduction theory is a historic mistake—a cowardly decision based on his inability to withstand the hostility of his colleagues.[21] For Krüll, it is a mistake made because Freud is unable to live with a theory that incriminates his father (Krüll, 40–58). And for most recovered-memory proponents, it is a mistake because it buries the reality of sexual child abuse beneath the primacy of fantasy.

This debate over Freud's change of mind is not yet settled, nor is it likely to be in the foreseeable future.[22] The difficulty in assessing the change is that there is very little factual detail. No case histories of the 18 patients have survived, or at least none have turned up. It thus becomes a matter of either being persuaded or not by Freud's four reasons for dropping the seduction theory. Masson even doubts that Freud was persuaded by his reasons.

My view is that Freud was overhasty in going public with claims he could not yet substantiate. His claims in "Heredity and the Aetiology of the Neuroses" that he has found sexual seduction in every case and has obtained therapeutic success is refuted by his admission to Fliess that he has not completed a single treatment. What Freud had was a hypothesis based on some cases where the seduction could be confirmed (*Freud-Fliess,* 43, 149). He then began to look for the same etiology in other cases in which he confidently (too confidently) expected to find it. Yet, as he admits in "Heredity and the Aetiology of the Neuroses," the patients "never repeat these stories spontaneously," and it requires "energetic pressure of the analytic procedure" to awaken them (*SE,* 3:153). Did Freud finally begin to worry about suggestion? He addresses this subject explicitly in a letter of 12 November 1897 (three months after the letter giving his four reasons for abandoning the seduction theory) when he discusses the successful treatment of a young girl by another analyst who gave no hint to the patient of what was expected (*Freud-Fliess,* 286). Paul Robinson observes that, if Freud was not worried about contamination of the seduction stories by suggestion, "he certainly should have been"—particularly in view of his description of the energy required by the analyst to awaken such stories.[23]

I take it that Freud's four reasons for reevaluating the seduction theory were persuasive to him and not motivated by other than intellectual reasons. By the time he gave them he had good reason to doubt his earlier enthusiasm for this theory. But I say reevaluating because, though often forgotten in the heat of current controversies, Freud does not abandon the seduction theory. In *Three Essays on the Theory of Sexuality* he refers to seduction as one of the external contingencies influencing sexual development and observes that he cannot admit that the views in "The Aetiology of Hysteria" exaggerated the frequency or importance of that influence, "though I did not then know that persons who remain normal may have had the same experiences in their childhood" (*SE,* 7:190). I would add, further, that persons without such experiences in childhood may become neurotic, and that the seduction theory cannot account for this fact. Freud's emerging concepts of infantile sexuality and the repressed unconscious enable him to account for neurosis where there is seduction and where there is no seduction. Needless to say, many of his critics do not agree that either view accounts for neurosis.

One thing, however, remains unchanged—the central role of sexuality. Why does Freud focus on this one element? After all, an incompatible idea could theoretically be anything rejected by the ego. In Freud's time, sexuality was likely to have been prominent among such incompatible ideas, but there were others (ambition, revenge, hate) that could also conflict with the ego. I think that sexuality as an etiological agent appealed to Freud for several reasons. For one thing the idea of sexual trauma gives him an event that possesses the relevant *"suitability to serve as a determinant"* and that possesses the necessary *"traumatic force"* (*SE,* 3:193; Freud's italics). It takes, he insists, more than simple fright to produce a conversion symptom. The seduction theory gives Freud an event that is both suitable and traumatic enough to cause a symptom. It also gives him something for which all clinicians of his time were looking in all diseases—a specific, concrete, tangible etiology, something as close to a disease-causing bacterium as he could get. The replacement of the seduction theory with the concept of sexual impulses in childhood does not alter these two points.

But these are clinical matters. I believe that sexuality is important for Freud in another way. In a letter of 30 June 1896, he writes that he longs to find the "solid ground on which I can cease to give psychological explanations and begin to find a physiological foundation!" Two years later (10 March 1898) he writes that his "theory of wish fulfillment has brought only the psychological solution and not the biological" (*Freud-Fliess,* 193, 301). Sometime during his self-analysis Freud had a dream in which Brücke assigned him the task of dissecting his own (Freud's) pelvis and legs. Alexander Grinstein sees one of the many themes of this dream as a fear of Brücke's reaction to Freud's psychological conclusions, "which could not be expressed in accordance with the laws that his teacher had set down for him."[24] Freud, in short, was troubled that he was leaving behind the firm organic base of his scientific training for the soft realm of merely psychological explanation. Sexuality, grounded as it was in the body, offered him a way to retain that organic base, whether in the physiology of his teacher or the evolution of Darwin. The importance of sexuality, then, was not arrived at entirely by objective clinical observation. For Freud, sexuality was a subject that allowed him to keep a foot in both camps and to preserve a sense of himself as a natural scientist. The "concept of instinct," he says in one of his many definitions, is "one of those lying on the frontier between the mental and the physical" (*SE,* 7:168).

The Theorist

So far I have concentrated on Freud as a clinical theorist. Yet he also remains a scientific theorist with a need to ground his clinical ideas in the organic. Given that need and his deep commitment to Brücke's teachings, it is no surprise to find that, along with various clinical activities in the 1890s, he also found time for a more thoroughgoing theoretical work. The result of this work is the *Project for a Scientific Psychology* (1895)—written in two or three weeks but unfinished and unpublished during Freud's lifetime. The almost one-hundred-page manuscript was found among Freud's letters to Fliess and first published in 1950.

Freud's intention in the *Project* is "to furnish a psychology that shall be a natural science: that is, to represent psychical processes as quantitatively determinate states of specifiable material particles, thus making those processes perspicuous and free from contradiction." The material particles are neurons (then newly discovered). Neurons may either be empty or charged with a variable quantity of energy, which distinguishes activity from rest and which is subject to the "general laws of motion" (*SE,* 1:295). The tendency of neurons is to discharge this quantity, which Freud calls the "principle of neuronal inertia" (296). Thus the nervous system attempts to keep the sum of excitation constant. External stimuli are more easily discharged than endogenous ones, which arise continuously from the body (hunger, respiration, sexuality) and from which the organism cannot flee. These endogenous stimuli are clearly an early version of the drives.[25]

Though abandoned after a few weeks because Freud could not develop the idea of purposive defense in a mechanical model (and probably also because he realized neuroscience was inadequate to the task he had undertaken), the work nevertheless introduces certain basic ideas and terms that will reappear in chapter 7 of *The Interpretation of Dreams* (1900), which is Freud's first major theoretical work in psychoanalysis. In fact, the *Project* throws much light on that complex chapter. Strachey even thinks (as I do) that the "*Project,* or rather its invisible ghost, haunts the whole series of Freud's theoretical writings to the very end" (290). The constancy principle is here (though not by that name). So are the primary and secondary processes, the idea of dreams as wish fulfillments, the idea of free and bound energy, and the idea of regression.

The *Project* represents in an extreme way Freud's commitment to a mechanistic physiology. In later works, as Wollheim aptly says, clinical findings interact with the "presuppositions retained from neurology" (Wollheim, 4). The basic presuppositions left over from neurology are the constancy principle, the idea of a passive central nervous system reflexly seeking discharge of all excitation, and the idea of inescapable endogenous energy that inexorably presses on the central nervous system and must be discharged in order to avoid unpleasure. The economic point of view, which deals with the distribution of psychic energy and which is central to Freud's understanding of neurosis and other psychic events, always implies these three elements. In later works, however, the economic view is balanced by other, more clinical points of view so that these works are characterized by "their curious and deliberate running together of the language of meaning and the language of causal process."[26]

Daniel Yankelovich and William Barrett suggest that Freud could have avoided this closed-system, Newtonian view (that is, force or energy moving material particles) of a complex nervous system that evolved only to find a way to escape stimuli. With a more Darwinian view, they surmise, he might at least have considered that the human nervous system evolved in a search for new stimuli. "Human mobility and restlessness," they say, "are blazoned on the pages of history, and it is hard to see how they could be the product of a nervous system whose essential function is to diminish stimuli, and if possible to eliminate them altogether" (Yankelovich and Barrett, 43).

This is interesting speculation about an unanswerable question. Could Freud have been a better Darwinian than he was and would that have affected his basic scientific position? Ritvo, I think, implies something like a positive answer in her contrast between Claus's Darwinism and Brücke's focus on the organism as an isolated unit of energy. Brücke's physiology and Claus's evolution, she suggests, did not necessarily interact, and Freud got more physiology than he did evolution (Ritvo, 161–69). Still, there is no way to know how Freud would have changed (if at all) from a more thorough and ongoing exposure to evolution than he had. What is certain is that he brought into his own theoretical thinking in the *Project* a view of the central nervous system as a passive organ that does not generate its own activity and implicitly retained this view even after he had substituted psychological for neurophysiological categories. Yet, in fact, as Robert Holt says, the "nervous system is perpetually *active,*" as demonstrated by electroencephalographic data (128; Holt's italics). From the standpoint of contemporary neuroscience, the idea of a passive brain whose activity must be initiated by energy from either external or internal (bodily) sources—the physiological basis for Freud's model of the mind—is entirely outmoded.

Self-Analysis

In mid-June 1896 Freud's father (age 81) became ill. He died in October. Freud wrote to Fliess on 2 November 1896, "the whole past has been awakened by this event." "I now feel quite uprooted," he concludes. In this same letter he encloses a "nice dream" he had the night of the funeral and that was clearly triggered by it. The dream, he says, "stems from the inclination to self reproach that regularly sets in among survivors" (*Freud-Fliess,* 202). I take this dream as the germ of Freud's self-analysis, on which he is fully engaged by 1897. "The chief patient I am preoccupied with is myself," he observes on 5 August 1897 (261). And on 14 November he writes that my self-analysis "suddenly started" (279). Clearly Freud's need to explore his feelings about his past and his father was a deeply personal one. It may have been additionally motivated by a wish to understand his own neurotic symptoms (cardiac symptoms and travel phobia, for example). But it was also slow and painful. He writes of "days when I drag myself about dejected because I have understood nothing of the dream, of the fantasy, of the mood of the day; and then again days when a flash of lightning illuminates the interrelations and lets me understand the past as a preparation for the present" (274). Thus Freud encounters the resistance he had already met in his patients.

The result of this self-analysis is Freud's discovery of his hostility toward his dead brother, Julius (the second child); the roots of his need for a friend and enemy who was the same person in his relationship with his nephew, John; and his Oedipal rivalry with his father and love of his mother. Indeed, Freud first mentions the Oedipus complex on 15 October 1897 (less than a month after the letter questioning the seduction theory), when he notes that "I have found, in my own case too, [the phenomenon of] being in love with my mother and jealous of my father." This letter contains his first association of this complex with Sophocles' *Oedipus Rex* and the first reference to the most famous psychoanalytic interpretation of a literary work in this century—that of Shakespeare's *Hamlet* (272). Eventually this autobiographical material found its way into *The Interpretation of Dreams* in the form of Freud's own dreams and his analysis of them. In his preface to the second edition of this book, Freud comments on the "subjective significance" of the book for him—"a significance which I only grasped after I had completed it." For it contains "a portion of my own self-analysis, my reaction to my father's death—that is to say, to the most important event, the most poignant loss, of a man's life" (*SE,* 4:xxvi). *An Autobiographical Study* is Freud's life presented objectively. *The Interpretation of Dreams* is his true autobiography.[27]

Freud's self-analysis was, of course, conducted alone. But he did have a listener who, though not his analyst, was nevertheless the recipient of many of Freud's confidences about what he had discovered about himself and his past. I refer to Wilhelm Fliess and to the letters Freud wrote to him from 1897 to 1900. I have referred to the Fliess letters frequently so far but have said nothing about him. As the successor to Freud's friendship with Breuer, he is too important in Freud's life to leave unmentioned.

Fliess was a Berlin ear, nose, and throat specialist. The two met in Vienna in 1887 when Fliess, in town for postgraduate study, was introduced to Freud by Breuer. They were attracted to each other and began to correspond that year. By 1892 the formal *Sie* (you) had become the informal *Du.* In the 1890s—especially after 1895, when Freud's relationship with Breuer was cooling off—the friendship deepened. The two men continued to write and to exchange ideas and drafts of papers. They also met frequently in different German or Austrian cities to discuss their mutual interests and developing ideas. They referred to their meetings as "congresses."

Fliess's ideas centered on the nose and human sexuality and the idea of a biological periodicity that ruled human life. From the first of these interests came his theory of the nasal reflex neurosis. From the second came his idea of a 28-day female and a 24-day male period in both sexes (which led him to the idea of human bisexuality). His goal was to create a biology based on these two periodicities.[28]

Fliess was the only man with whom Freud shared his ideas in the 1890s, the only man to whom he could say virtually anything and everything. He became Freud's sounding board, as Freud presumably became his (his letters to Freud have not been found). How far Freud approved of Fliess's bizarre ideas is uncertain, but from the letters in which Freud plays around with Fliess's periodicities it would appear that for a while he took them seriously (*Freud-Fliess,* 209–11). Certainly the nasal reflex neurosis interested Freud—enough, in fact, for him to allow Fliess to operate on the nose of his patient, Emma Eckstein (1865–1924), with disastrous results. Fliess left surgical gauze in the nasal cavity after the surgery. On removal of the gauze there was massive hemorrhage and a real danger that Emma might die.[29] Fortunately she recovered and eventually became the first woman to practice psychoanalysis.

For many psychoanalysts this episode and the whole Fliess relationship is an embarrassment. Evidently it was for Freud also, as he vigorously opposed the publication of his letters when they were found in the 1930s. Still, it is worth remembering that, during the period when Freud was trying to solve the riddle of the neuroses and during his self-analysis, Fliess was the person who made it possible for Freud to talk to someone other than himself and so to work out his ideas with some kind of audience. He also gave Freud the idea of human bisexuality. By 1904 both the correspondence and the friendship were over, apparently because of a growing intellectual tension between the two men.

Chapter Three

The First Psychoanalyst (1900–1913)

In the period now under consideration Freud emerges as the first psychoanalyst. The period begins with *The Interpretation of Dreams* (published 4 November 1899 but bearing the date 1900) and ends with *Totem and Taboo* (1913), Freud's first major application of psychoanalysis to another discipline—in this case, anthropology. Between 1900 and 1905 he published three of the fundamental texts of psychoanalysis: *The Psychopathology of Everyday Life* (1901), *Three Essays on the Theory of Sexuality* (1905), and *Jokes and Their Relation to the Unconscious* (1905). In these 13 years he also published four of his five major case histories, the first published psychoanalytic reading of a literary work ("Delusions and Dreams in Jensen's *Gradiva*"), the first psychoanalytic psychobiography ("Leonardo da Vinci and a Memory of His Childhood"), a major theoretical paper ("Formulations on the Two Principles of Mental Functioning"), and other essays on a variety of clinical and nonclinical subjects. My emphasis in this chapter is on the works of this period that are central to psychoanalytic theory and therapy. I refer to other works as they relate to this emphasis.

Theory and Interpretation of Dreams

In a letter to Fliess on 6 August 1899, Freud says of *The Interpretation of Dreams* that the "whole thing is planned on the model of an imaginary walk." At the beginning there is "the dark forest of authors" who are "hopelessly lost on wrong tracks." Then comes a "concealed pass through which I lead the reader—my specimen dream with its peculiarities, details, indiscretions, bad jokes—and then suddenly the high ground and the view and the question: which way do you wish to go now?" (*Freud-Fliess,* 365). Leonard Shengold and Stanley Edgar Hyman have written of the literary structure of the book implied in this letter. For both, the dominant metaphor is that of a journey, and this journey is accompanied by appropriate allusions to other famous literary journeys—those of Aeneas (the epigraph to the book is from Virgil), Oedipus, Dante. As Hyman says, "Freud is a mythic hero who has made the dangerous journey into the underworld and come back with the treasure, and in this aspect the book's form is that of a successful mythic quest."[1]

In addition to being autobiography and mythic narrative, however, *The Interpretation of Dreams* is also a scientific treatise on the psychology of dreams and a book on how to interpret dreams. It divides quite naturally into these two parts. The first six chapters are on the interpretation of dreams. Chapter 7, the last chapter, is a theory of the psychology of dreams. Freud is fully aware of this division. Early in the seventh chapter he observes that "the problems of dream-interpretation have hitherto occupied the centre of the picture," but this chapter will "endeavor to penetrate more deeply into the mental process involved in dreaming" (*SE,* 5:510–11). Dream interpretation and dream psychology, then, are the related yet separable subjects of *The Interpretation of Dreams.*

On dream interpretation Freud announces his intention in the opening sentence. He will bring forward "proof that there is a psychological technique which makes it possible to interpret dreams" and will show with that technique that every dream is a "psychical structure which has a meaning and which can be inserted at an assignable point in the mental activities of waking life" (*SE,* 4:1).

After a long introductory chapter in which he reviews other theories of dreams, Freud proceeds in the second chapter to give a sample dream analysis of one of his own dreams. The dream is Freud's first analyzed dream (24 July 1895) and is probably the most famous dream of the century. He calls it simply "Dream of July 23rd–24th, 1895" (107). It is usually called the dream of Irma's injection. The dream takes place in a large hall where the Freuds are giving a reception. Among the guests is Irma, whom Freud reproaches for not yet having accepted his solution to her illness. Irma complains about pains in her throat, stomach, and abdomen. Freud looks into her mouth and sees a large white patch and curly structures. He then calls Dr. M., who repeats and confirms the examination. Now two other doctors appear, Freud's friends Otto and Leopold, who percusses Irma's chest and finds a dull area in the left lower lung. Dr. M. diagnoses an infection, after which the origin of the infection becomes clear. Otto had given Irma a preparation of "*propyl, propyls . . . propionic acid . . . trimethylamin (and I saw before me the formula for this printed in heavy type),*" and the syringe had probably not been clean (107; Freud's italics).

In the rest of this chapter Freud analyzes the dream by his preferred method. He takes each line of the written dream and tries to discuss what association it brings to mind—a process that takes 14 pages. Thus, as he says, the meaning of the dream became apparent. The day before the dream Otto had said to Freud that Irma was better but not well. Freud took this as a reproach. The dream, then, represented a conscious thought about Irma's (and several other peoples') health, and acquitted Freud of the responsibility for Irma's condition. The dream, Freud concludes, "represented a particular state of affairs as I should have wished it to be" (118–19). Its content and its motive was a wish. He is now ready for his first formulation: "*When the work of interpretation has been completed, we perceive that a dream is the fulfilment of a wish*" (121; Freud's italics).

In the third chapter Freud enlarges on the idea of dreams as wish-fulfilling by discussing two kinds of dreams. First, there are dreams of adults, which transparently express wishes. Second, there are the dreams of children, which also transparently express wishes. In children's dreams, moreover, there is not simply a wish for something. The dream represents the wish as actually fulfilled. But now he must confront an obvious objection, which is that many (perhaps most) dreams do not fulfill a wish in any obvious way. Many dreams, indeed, contain much distressing material with no sign of a wish. He has an answer: such dreams are distorted or disguised, so that the dream must be interpreted (decoded) in order to detect the underlying wish. So he introduces the distinction between the manifest and latent content of dreams (135). The manifest dream is the one remembered and reported by the dreamer. The latent content is the wishes that have produced the dream and that, because they may be disturbing, must be distorted into the manifest dream. The distortion occurs as a defensive reaction of one agency (the censor) against a wish arising from another agency (here unnamed). Much of the fourth chapter is devoted to an often overingenious interpretation of dreams into their wishful origin. Freud concludes with a variation on his initial formula: "*A dream is a (disguised) fulfilment of a (suppressed or repressed) wish*" (160; Freud's italics).

In the fifth chapter Freud turns to the materials and sources of the manifest dream and focuses on four kinds of material. First, there is what he calls recent and indifferent material, which is always some experience of the previous day but may also come from several days (occasionally even further) back. The previous day's residue, he argues, is an invariable feature of every dream (this is confirmed by contemporary dream research). Second, there is infantile material. Even though the manifest dream may only allude to this infantile material, such material is frequent in dreams. As he says, "*we find the child and the child's impulses still living on in the dream*" (191; Freud's italics). In this section, Freud includes an analysis of some of his own dreams with infantile material, many of them—the Count Thun dream, the Rome dreams, and the dream of the three Fates—containing very rich autobiographical material. Third, Freud considers somatic sources (that is, external or internal stimuli) of dreams. Though he agrees that such stimuli (alarm clocks, hunger, noises of various kinds) can affect dreams, he does not agree that the "wealth of ideational material in dreams" is due to such somatic material (221).

The fourth subject Freud considers in this chapter is typical dreams—dreams that are dreamt by almost everyone and may possibly have the same meaning for everyone. These include examination dreams, dreams of being naked, and flying dreams. But the important typical dream for Freud is that of the death of loved ones—brothers, sisters, and parents especially. In the case of parents, he observes, the dead parent is usually of the same sex as the dreamer, and there is no doubt that such dreams are a wish for the death of that parent. They are Oedipal dreams, and it is in this section that Freud first refers publicly to *Oedipus Rex* (and also *Hamlet*) as a literary analogy to these kinds of dreams. Already he is convinced that the "chief part in the mental lives of all children who later become psychoneurotics is played by their parents" (260).

In the sixth chapter, the longest of the book, Freud turns to what he calls the dream work. The manifest dream and the latent dream thoughts, he says, are like two different languages for the same subject. While the latent thoughts are immediately comprehensible "as soon as we have learnt them," the manifest dream is like a picture puzzle or rebus and must always appear nonsensical unless read according to its symbolic relationship to the latent thoughts (277–78). There must, therefore, be some kind of process by which the one is transformed into the other, and this he calls the dream work. He identifies five mechanisms by which this work of defensive transformation is performed: condensation, displacement, representability, symbolism, and secondary revision.

Condensation is the process that accounts for the brevity of dreams, the sense of compression. It is brought about by omission of some of the dream thoughts so that the manifest dream is only a fragment of the full dream. It may work by highlighting one image that then becomes a nodal point leading by association to multiple dream thoughts. Freud uses the botanical monograph in his dream of that name to show how many dream thoughts converged on this one image (282–84). In other cases condensation produces collective or composite figures, as in the Irma dream where Irma represents Freud's eldest daughter, an unnamed lady, a patient of Freud's who had died of poisoning, a child from the neurological clinic, and Freud's wife (292). Fusing as it does one or more dream thoughts into a single image, condensation is one of the reasons dreams are overdetermined—that is, that they usually have more than one meaning. Thus, association from an image in the manifest dream leads to diverging associations that in turn lead to several different dream thoughts.

Displacement means the shifting of identity in dreams from significant to insignificant material so that what is significant is either replaced or only alluded to by what is insignificant. Again the botanical monograph dream is relevant: in the dream he simply sees a monograph in a bookstore window; the dream thought to which he is led by association is emotionally loaded since it concerns his self-justification as a doctor (about which he is considerably anxious). The consequence of displacement, he says, is that the dream content does not resemble the dream thought, so that the dream "gives no more than a distortion of the dream-wish which exists in the unconscious." Distortion, of course, means the censor, and indeed Freud says that displacement is one of the "chief methods by which that distortion is achieved" (308). The insignificant element can escape the censor, the significant one cannot.

By consideration of representability Freud means that the dream must portray words or abstract ideas in visual images. Anything that can be made pictorial, then, can be represented in a dream. Visual images in dreams do not represent logical relations or critical thought activity. Logical connection becomes simultaneity in time; causal relations become a temporal sequence (as in two related dreams). Sometimes representation involves exchanges of similar-sounding words and puns, so dreams are often witty and may appear to be making jokes.

The fourth mechanism of the dream work, symbolism, is absent from the first edition of *The Interpretation of Dreams.* In the 1909 and 1911 editions, however, Freud adds material on symbolism in dreams and, in 1914, that material becomes a section in the chapter on the dream work. In *Introductory Lectures on Psycho-Analysis* (1917) he discusses symbolism in dreams in a full lecture, which, as Strachey says, may be Freud's most important writing on that subject (*SE,* 15:149). Symbols,

Freud says here, do not vary from dreamer to dreamer. They are constant, "stable translations" (151). The range of things symbolized "is not wide: the human body as a whole, parents, children, brothers and sisters, birth, death, nakedness—and something else besides" (153). Charles Rycroft objects to Freud's statement that the things symbolized are not wide. For, he argues, in fact Freud's list "covers an extremely wide range of human experience, almost everything indeed apart from work, play and intellectual activity." He argues that in dreams the range of things symbolized "embraces all aspects of man's life-cycle—and that the study of dreams reveals that human beings are more preoccupied with their biological destiny than most of them realize."[2]

By "and something else besides," of course, Freud means sexual life, which, as Rycroft knows, he wants to emphasize. Sexual life includes the genitals, sexual processes, and sexual intercourse. The main part of Freud's lecture consists of a listing of symbols for the male and female genitals. The symbols reflect an obvious comparison based on shape—elongated objects for the male genitals, enclosing or hollow objects for the female genitals (that is, knives, sticks, trees and so on as against pits, vessels, cupboards and so on). These are the famous Freudian symbols of popular culture, known far and wide by people who have never read a word of his writings. Interestingly, Freud notes that his evidence for the meaning of symbols is not clinical (his patients do not usually know the meaning of symbols and are unable to associate to them) but extraclinical—from a study of fairy tales, myths, jokes, folklore, and poetic and colloquial usage (*SE,* 15:158–59). He also notes that symbolic interpretation (which smacks of the old dream books) cannot replace free association, which remains the preferred method of dream interpretation.

Finally, there is secondary revision, "whose business it is to make something whole and more or less coherent out of the first products of the dream-work" (182). Because of secondary revision, a person reporting a dream makes it more coherent and consistent than it was. Secondary revision, as Freud says, is a kind of first interpretation before "being submitted to waking interpretation" (*SE,* 5:490).[3]

By the end of this long chapter on the dream work, Freud has accomplished his two purposes: to show a technique of dream interpretation and to show that dreams are meaningful. But dream interpretation is not enough for him. He wants to study dreams scientifically (which is not the same thing as interpretation), and, beyond that, he wants to use a theory of dreams as a way of approaching a theory of the mind. Hence chapter 7, "The Psychology of the Dream-Processes." To move from the first six chapters of *The Interpretation of Dreams* to this chapter is (for me) to move to a different book. The first six chapters are not very technical. Chapter 7 is highly speculative and abstract. This chapter is unquestionably the theoretical foundation of psychoanalysis. As it is over a hundred pages long, however, I will necessarily be highly selective in what I can say about it.

The first thing to note is that Freud is talking about psychical locality, which means he is not concerned with anatomy. "I shall remain upon psychological ground," he says (536). Thus, when he speaks of psychical agencies or systems, or when he describes stimuli passing from the sensory to the motor end of the psychic (or mental) apparatus, he implies no location of such processes in the brain. All of his spatial images are ways of picturing a psychological process detached from anatomy. Or so he says. The publication of the *Project* suggests that he has not completely left his neuropathology behind. He simply restates it in psychological terms. Sometimes he even slips back into the language of neurology, as when he asserts that the "nervous system [not the psychic apparatus] is an apparatus which has the function of getting rid of stimuli that reach it, or of reducing them to the lowest possible level; or which, if it were feasible, would maintain itself in an altogether unstimulated condition" (*SE,* 14:120). Moreover, like the central nervous system of the *Project,* the psychic apparatus is pictured as reflexly receiving and discharging external and internal stimuli.

Second, for the first time Freud presents the unconscious as a system. What he has hitherto described as the unconscious or unconscious mental processes is now the system Ucs. In a spatial image Freud locates system Ucs. at the motor end of the sensorimotor reflex arc and states that stimuli moving from perception toward motor response must pass through this system. Between perception and the system Ucs. lie the memory or *mnemic* systems of varying levels of abstraction through which perception is processed prior to a motor response and that contain permanent traces of previous perceptions associatively linked. Between the system Ucs. and a motor response lies the system Pcs. (preconscious). Thus, system Ucs. has no access to consciousness except through the preconscious, and in traversing the preconscious it is "obliged to submit to modifications" (*SE,* 5:541).

Such, then, is the topographical view of the mind—a view that will remain fundamentally unaltered until *The Ego and the Id* (1923). The topography is tripartite: consciousness, the preconscious (Pcs.), and the unconscious (Ucs.). Stimuli moving from the preconscious to consciousness can do so freely. Stimuli moving from the unconscious to the preconscious cannot do so without distortion (that is, they are repressed). Yet these unconscious stimuli can still affect behavior, for the fact that they are unconscious does not mean they are weak. Indeed, they are strong and active, as Freud had learned from Bernheim in regard to posthypnotic suggestion (an experience that he repeatedly uses as giving him his first glimpse of the effect of unconscious ideas on behavior). This way of representing the relationship between system Ucs. and system Pcs. Freud calls the dynamic view (610). For Freud the topographical view is only descriptive (though still useful). But the dynamic view, as Wollheim points out, is an addition to our knowledge, not just our vocabulary, because it compels recognition that "dynamically unconscious events are required in the explanation, not simply in the redescription, of certain forms of behavior" (Wollheim, 179). In general the unconscious is the "larger sphere, which includes within it the smaller sphere of the conscious" (*SE,* 5:612).[4] Obviously, the unconscious is for Freud not a philosophical concept but a psychical reality.

But topography and dynamics describe the relationship of unconscious and preconscious. Freud also wants to understand the processes that characterize and differentiate each system. This he attempts to do in his distinction between the primary and secondary processes—for many analysts the most essential contribution of psychoanalysis to psychology. Basically, Freud discovers that the mind functions in two different ways. First presented in the *Project* as neuronal processes, in *The Interpretation of Dreams* they are presented as psychical processes (588–609), though, as Fancher observes, only slightly modified from their first appearance (Fancher 1973, 127). In "Formulations on the Two Principles of Mental Functioning" (1911), he defines them as principles—that is, not just as different levels of activity but two alien modes of activity (*SE,* 12:218–26).

The primary process is the mode of operation of the system Ucs.[5] It is the original, most primitive mode of mental functioning in the infant and is characterized by Freud as having a mobility of cathexis (energy is unbound) that leads to condensation and displacement, a tendency to transfer intensity to intermediate ideas rather than stressing the right one, a loose association in the relations among ideas (often based on homonyms and verbal similarities), and a tolerance of mutually contradictory ideas such as love and hate for the same person (*SE,* 5:595–97).[6] Since dreams exhibit all of these characteristics, they are, Freud concludes, primarily a product of the unconscious. The primary process operates according to the unpleasure principle—that is, it acts so as to avoid an accumulation of excitation, which is felt as unpleasure, and seeks to diminish any such accumulation (598).[7] This, of course, is the principle of tension reduction now brought into a psychological context. It is important to note that the need to diminish excitation is immediate, peremptory, and without regard for reality.

The primary process, and hence the unconscious, can only wish. His explanation of this surprising fact derives from the fiction (his word) of a primitive psychical apparatus "whose activities are regulated by an effort to avoid an accumulation of excitation and to maintain itself so far as possible without excitation" (598).[8] To illustrate a wish, Freud imagines a hungry baby who experiences an internal need from which it is impossible to flee and that causes unpleasure. The baby has a "mnemic image" of previous experiences of satisfaction (that is, of receiving nourishment). When hungry the next time a "psychical impulse" emerges that attempts to "re-establish the situation of the original satisfaction." The impulse to recreate this situation is what Freud calls a wish. Wishing ends in a hallucinatory repetition of the perception (feeding at the breast) "which was linked with the satisfaction of the need." The fulfilled wish allows momentary satisfaction—that is, a discharge of tension.

But only momentarily. The baby will get hungry again and, in any case, a hallucinated breast does not nourish. Primitive thought activity must bow to reality, to what Freud calls the "bitter experience of life" (565–66). A secondary process is required to satisfy needs realistically.[9] The needs persist but, under the sway of the secondary process, are deferred or inhibited until they can be realistically satisfied. In the secondary process, then, energy is bound, attention is focused on external reality, and thinking becomes verbal and logical. From the point of view of the conscious and logical secondary process, many of the wishes of the primary process (taking mother away from father, for example, or the death of a loved one) are no longer pleasurable because they are condemned by the dominant mass of ideas of society. The fulfillment of such wishes, says Freud, no longer generates "an affect of pleasure but of unpleasure," and it is this "*transformation of affect which constitutes the essence of what we term 'repression'* " (604; Freud's italics). Yet these wishes persist in dreams and in neurotics who, frustrated by reality, attempt to find pleasure in what have become conflict-filled and unrealistic earlier modes of satisfaction.

The secondary process (the preconscious) can also wish, as we see in Freud's Irma dream, where he wishes to be vindicated as a doctor.

Wishes aroused during the day of the dream and not satisfied or else repudiated constitute much of the content of the day's residue in the latent dream thought. For Freud, however, such wishes (which could, after all, become conscious in waking life) are not sufficient to produce a dream. A conscious wish can only instigate a dream if it awakens an unconscious wish and receives reinforcement (that is, unbound psychic energy) from it. An unconscious wish, on the other hand, can instigate a dream on its own.[10] He never abandons the view that "*a wish which is represented in a dream must be an infantile one*" (553; Freud's italics).[11] These infantile wishes remain the "core of our being" and remain inaccessible both to understanding and complete inhibition by the secondary process (603).

This is why a dream is a compromise formation. Unconscious wishes pressing for satisfaction cannot appear directly in a dream, for this would disturb the wish of the preconscious to sleep. For Freud we dream in order to sleep. To remain asleep and in order to evade the censor the wishes must be disguised by the dream work. Because of the censorship (and also because motor activity is inhibited in sleep and consciousness is withdrawn from the external world) the wish cannot move toward consciousness. It is forced along a regressive path from the motor to the perceptual system of the mental apparatus and is changed into a sensory image. In other words, it moves from secondary to primary process and is perceived as the hallucinatory fulfillment of a repressed infantile wish that is typically egoistic, sexual, or aggressive and that does not necessarily reflect the conscious relationship to the persons in the dream.

Dream Theory Today

Freud's idea of dreams as a royal road to the unconscious is the beginning of a long tradition of the interpretation of dreams in the twentieth century. In his survey of dream interpreters who have agreed, partially agreed, or disagreed with Freud, Richard Jones mentions Carl Jung, Alfred Adler, Herbert Silberer, Samuel Lowy, Calvin Hall, Thomas French, Montague Ullman, Erik Erikson, and Medard Boss.[12] *The Interpretation of Dreams* is foundational in this tradition but, given the amount of disagreement among the people on this list, certainly not the last word.

Laboratory dream research has also contributed to a revaluation of *The Interpretation of Dreams*. Since the observation in 1955 of REM (rapid eye movement) sleep, the study of the physiology of dreams has become an important field of research. REM periods occur about every 90 minutes during the night. Subjects awakened during such periods (as monitored by electroencephalograph) report that they were dreaming. Thus, in human beings REM sleep is associated with dreaming.[13] From the point of view of REM sleep, we sleep in order to dream rather than dream in order to sleep. So dreams are not, as Freud thinks, the guardians of sleep.

What is important in terms of Freud's dream theory is that REM periods initiate dreaming, not the reverse. In his activation-synthesis hypothesis, J. Allan Hobson sees the dreaming process as originating in the brain stem by randomly initiated information signals that eventually reach the cortex, which then tries to order these signals into a meaningful synthetic pattern.[14] This may not be the final word on dream physiology, but it does reinforce the point that a physiological state, not a repressed wish, instigates dreaming. Wish fulfillment, as Jones says, now becomes a consequence, not a cause, of dreams (Jones 1970, 120–21). But then, as Wilma Bucci has recently argued, a dream may equally contain consequences other than unconscious wishes, "a fear, worry, or conflict, or a problem the individual is trying to solve"—all those matters, in other words, which Freud subordinated to the repressed infantile wish.[15]

The change in regard to Freud's view of wish as the cause and deepest interpretation of a dream is already a significant revision. To question the wish hypothesis, however, is also to question Freud's idea of dream distortion. For he needed the idea of disguise in order to argue for the existence of a latent wish. REM-state research, as Paul Kline observes in a survey of that research, reveals the manifest dream as more important than in Freud's view.[16] To emphasize the manifest dream is to downplay, if not eliminate, the latent dream thought. Hobson, for example, argues that dreams are "rather transparent and unedited"—echoing, as he recognizes, Jung's long-held view that dreams are "transparently meaningful" (Hobson, 214).[17] For many, the transparency of a dream's meaning is a settled matter, and they discard (sometimes even mock) Freud's convenient censor who is always ready when needed. Jones thinks that Freud's view of neurotic symptoms as a compromise formation based on defense led him to postulate the same structure for dreams (Jones 1970, 18–20). He has a point, for Freud constantly draws analogies between dreams and neuroses in *The Interpretation of Dreams.* Yet, as Harry Hunt says, we may not want to turn too quickly from the idea of disguise in dreams to an " 'open window' " metaphor. If disguise occurs in waking life (normal and neurotic) and if dreams are a mode of thought, then people "may well dream much as they communicate with others" (Hunt, 36).

At issue behind the displacement of repressed infantile wishes as dream instigators and of disguise as a defining feature of dreams is the basic theory that led Freud to these two views. I refer to the related ideas of the passive central nervous system and the tension reduction model. A repressed infantile wish is for Freud the psychic representative of an internal, continuously active instinctual impulse that enters the psyche as a demand for discharge. For Hobson, the "energy that activates the brain during REM sleep is neuronal, and the neuron is able to create its own information." Moreover, because the brain can inhibit or cancel stimuli coming from inside or outside the body, it is not at the mercy of a continuously accumulating energy that is perceived as unpleasure (Hobson, 215).

Contemporary research into the physiology of dreams, I conclude, requires a reconsideration and probably a reformulation of Freud's theory of dreaming. What about dream interpretation? The essential issue in dream interpretation, says Hunt, is whether there are symbolic processes operating within the dream rather than inferred from the dream (Hunt, 9).[18] For Hobson, who does not deny that dreams have meaning, symbolic processes are minimal because the synthesis part of the activation-synthesis hypothesis is minimal. Hunt's massive survey of dream research from clinic to sleep laboratory to dreams in other cultures suggests that dream symbolism is more complex than Hobson would allow. And Bucci argues that, when divested of the elements of Freud's energy theory—that is, the idea of the energy of an unconscious wish, dreams as the guardians of sleep, the censor, the manifest content as a concealment of the actual meaning—dreams are an attempt to represent emotional meanings by a process of subsymbolic activation that becomes symbolic (Bucci, 247–63). The meaning of dreams—what they mean, how much they mean, and how to interpret them—will almost certainly continue to be a subject of debate and investigation for some time to come. In the meantime, Freud's discovery that dreams have meaning continues for many (including myself) to be a fundamental insight.

Misachievement in Everyday Life

The Psychopathology of Everyday Life appeared in 1901 and introduced to the world the Freudian slip. It is probably Freud's most popular book. It is certainly his most accessible one. No other book of Freud's is so free of technical terms or of abstruse theory as this one. Freud obviously understood the value of this absence of the technical when he used the mental phenomena treated in the book to begin his *Introductory Lectures on Psycho-Analysis* (published in 1917 but delivered during the 1915–16 winter term at the University of Vienna). This material was not only a simple introduction to psychoanalysis, but was also illustrative of Freud's idea of the continuity between normal and neurotic processes. Once he abandoned the view of the hereditary causation of neurosis, Freud never tired of emphasizing the connection between normal and pathological processes.

Freud's word for the phenomena treated in this book is *Fehlleistung,* which Strachey translates as faulty function but which can also be translated as misachievement. Strachey calls this bit of mischief a parapraxis—a neutral Latin term which implies a kind of scientific rigor not present in Freud's original formulation.[19] A misachievement is a kind of mischief people intentionally (but not necessarily consciously) bring on themselves. It is not a Latinate scientific concept that victimizes us against our will. This being said, however, I will adapt to general usage and refer to parapraxes.

The purpose of *The Psychopathology of Everyday Life,* Freud says, is to accumulate examples of parapraxes that support the idea of unconscious but active mental processes (*SE,* 6:272 n). He examines multiple phenomena, all of which must meet three criteria in order to qualify as parapraxes: they must be within normal limits, they must be temporary disturbances, and they must be without any apparent motive (239). Parapraxes include slips of the tongue (using a different word for the one intended), slips of the pen, misreading, and mishearing. They also include varieties of forgetting; some forgetting is temporary (names or an intention to do something), some forgetting is not temporary (mislaying or losing things). Other kinds of parapraxes include errors of belief, bungled actions, and symptomatic actions. Finally, parapraxes may be combined—that is, a symptomatic action such as missing an appointment may involve forgetting the time of the appointment.

The usual explanation for parapraxes, Freud observes, includes indisposition or fatigue, overexcitation, and preoccupation. Freud accepts each of these physical elements as capable of facilitating a parapraxis but not as causing one. After all, he says, parapraxes occur in the absence of any of these three elements. An explanation of parapraxes that involves language arises from philology. Freud examines the work of philologists who claim that transposition, anticipation, perseveration, and substitution of words may occur entirely on the basis of similarity of sound and syllable in words. Again, Freud agrees that these activities may be involved in the creation of verbal parapraxes but argues that they do not constitute the motive for such an error.

What does constitute a motive to produce a parapraxis? To answer this question Freud decides to look at the product itself rather than its possible physical or verbal causes. To look at the product, he argues, is to see that parapraxes have a sense, a purpose, an intention. Here, for example, is one of his favorite instances of a slip. The president of the Lower House of the Austrian Parliament is about to open the sitting. Gentlemen, he says, " 'I take notice that a full quorum is present and herewith declare the sitting *closed!*' " (59; Freud's italics). The mistake drew instant laughter. Freud observes that in addition to intending to open the Parliament the president reveals another wish counter to that intention—the wish that the Parliament was closed because little good could come of it.

There is, he notes, no verbal exchange in this slip, merely a replacement of one word by its opposite. In other cases verbal similarity can produce a composite word (a compromise formation as in dreams). For example, a young man addressed a young lady in the street by asking her if she would permit him to *begleit-digen* her—a meaningless word that combines *begleiten* (accompany) and *beleidigen* (insult). Two conflicting emotional impulses result in the slip, which, as Freud says (and the young woman understood at once) suggest that the young man's intentions were "not of the purest, and was bound to seem, even to himself, insulting to the lady" (68). Freud calls the impulse that intrudes on the intended word the disturbing thought or purpose and the conscious intention the disturbed thought or purpose. This model of disturbing and disturbed thought applies to all parapraxes, including nonverbal ones such as forgetting the appointment one does not really want to keep.

Not all disturbing thoughts are unconscious. Some are known even before the parapraxis, some are unknown before the parapraxis but understood immediately after, and others are vigorously rejected by the person and are thus truly unconscious. The last group can be understood and brought to consciousness only by free association, as in the interpretation of dreams or the treatment of neuroses.

Adolph Grünbaum's critique of Freud's view of parapraxes is especially directed at this third group. He takes Freud's famous example of the young man who forgets the Latin word *aliquis* when quoting a line from Virgil's *Aenead*: " 'Let someone [*aliquis*] arise from my bones as an avenger!' " The line expresses his bitterness toward the treatment of Jews and his wish for descendants to avenge him. He knows he has omitted a word from the line but cannot recall it. Freud then supplies the word and has the man free-associate to it. The chain of association (*a-liquis,* relics, liquifying, fluidity, fluid) leads to the man's anxiety that his lady friend is pregnant (she has missed her period), which is the disturbing thought interfering with the man's conscious wish for descendants (9–11).

For Grünbaum, there are two things wrong with Freud's interpretation. First, the reasoning is *post hoc, ergo propter hoc*—the belief that because one thing is followed by another, the first is the cause of the second. Second, thematic affinity by itself does not mean causal linkage. I should observe that Grünbaum's critique is not directed only at Freud's view of slips. It is intended as a part of his more general critique of free association as an adequate method of casual analysis.[20]

In his recent critique of Grünbaum, Donald Levy (like Grünbaum a philosopher, not a psychoanalyst) addresses these points. In his view, the "temporal order in which things are said and thought is surely meaningful and, very generally, causally significant." The order of words and ideas in human discourse usually implies a causal connection between earlier and later words and ideas. Moreover, thematic affinity between things generally implies a causal connection. It would, he says, "take heroic efforts of abstraction (probably unsuccessful) to listen to another person, suspending our strong 'bias' toward the assumption that the thematic affinities and temporal sequences in their words have a causal linkage."[21]

Another critic of Freud's account of slips is Sebastiano Timpanaro (whom Grünbaum cites approvingly). Timpanaro argues that most of the slips Freud discusses are simply the result of lapses of attention or of what he calls banalization, in which a familiar word is spoken or read instead of an unfamiliar one (as, for example, scribes do in transcribing a text).[22] Timpanaro has a point. Freud's belief in psychic determinism was adamantly held and led him to argue that even the apparently most trivial psychic activity (the selection of a number at random, say) was intentional and that its meaning was firmly rooted in the person's life. Hence all parapraxes were purposive, not accidental, for him. Still, I wonder if some of Timpanaro's bored or inattentive scribes did not experience momentary disturbing thoughts. In any case Timpanaro misses the contextual aspect of Freud's interpretations where he has access to the person involved. He always views the meaning of the parapraxis in terms of the person's current situation, concerns, feelings, and so on, never apart from them. His question, as Levy rightly says, is always Why did this person commit the parapraxis at this time? He then asserts that a mechanism discovered in a large number of cases applies universally, and perhaps this is an overstatement. But that doesn't mean Freud is not correct about a very large number of parapraxes.

Besides, not all parapraxes involve linguistic errors. Bungled actions—dropping, knocking over, and breaking objects or intentional self-injury—are mistakes in motor, not linguistic, behavior. So too are chance or symptomatic acts, such as a bride losing her wedding ring on the honeymoon or a wife accidentally signing a check in her maiden name. Then there are errors, such as accidentally dialing the number of one with whom we do not wish to speak. Finally, there are combined parapraxes, such as the man (Ernest Jones, in fact) who forgot to post a letter for several days, finally sent it off only to have it returned for lack of an address, and then took it back to the post with no stamp. It is hard to deny the unconsciously intentional nature of such acts, especially if on analysis they reveal motives in a person's life that corroborate their purposive sense. As Freud says, in every case of intentional forgetting, the motive is a feeling of unpleasure (136). A feeling of unpleasure is also the motive in those indifferent memories of childhood (what Freud calls screen memories) that are substitutes for significant and disturbing impressions (43–52).

Freud concludes *The Psychopathology of Everyday Life* by making the connection among dreams, neuroses, and parapraxes explicit. In both dreams and parapraxes, he says, we find condensation and other compromise formations. In both, "unconscious thoughts find expression as modifications of other thoughts." Neurotic symptoms, moreover, "repeat in their mechanisms" the essential mode of function of parapraxes and dreams. Thus, the borderline between the normal and the abnormal is "a fluid one," and we are "all a little neurotic." Indeed, parapraxes differ from neuroses only by the fact that they are located in the "least important psychical functions," whereas in neuroses the symptoms appear in the "most important individual and social functions and are able to disturb nutrition, sexual intercourse, professional work and social life." What is common to both is that "*the phenomena can be traced back to incompletely suppressed psychical material, which, although pushed away by consciousness, has nevertheless not been robbed of all capacity for expressing itself*" (278–79; Freud's italics).

On Jokes

In *Jokes and Their Relation to the Unconscious* (1905) Freud continues his study of a number of phenomena that are related by their similar mechanisms—dreams, parapraxes, and neuroses. Though nontechnical, this book can be difficult for an English reader because the jokes are mostly in German and the context of many of the jokes is now very distant.

Freud's formula for a joke is very simple: "*a preconscious thought is given over for a moment to unconscious revision and the outcome of this is at once grasped by conscious perception*" (*SE,* 8:166). Unconscious revision means primary process, and the second chapter on the technique of jokes (the joke work) describes the operation of condensation and displacement in creating them. Jokes involve verbal play of a kind favored by both condensation and displacement. Already an analogy with dreams is implied.

All jokes use the same verbal mechanisms, Freud argues, but not all jokes have the same purpose. There are nontendentious and tendentious jokes. Nontendentious jokes know no end but the verbal play itself. Freud likens this verbal play to that of children playing with words regardless of whether they make sense. Such verbal play is ended by the development of what Freud calls the "critical reason," which now rejects play as meaningless (126). Nontendentious jokes permit a recovery of this childhood sense of play and the pleasure it arouses and thus bring about a momentary respite from the burden of being critical or reasonable—or adult.

Tendentious jokes allow the same yield of pleasure, but they also serve another aim. In tendentious jokes, an aggressive, a sexual, a cynical, or a skeptical aim is the point of the joke. For such jokes there is pleasure from the verbal play but also pleasure from the experience of achieving these aims. Tendentious jokes, Freud says, use the verbal play as a kind of fore-pleasure in order that they "may produce new pleasure by lifting suppressions and repressions" (137). They make possible the satisfaction of an instinct suppressed or repressed by the pressure of civilization. The restraint imposed by civilization on sexuality and aggression is clear, but why cynicism and skepticism? Because, says Freud, these two attitudes also allow us to escape the burden of reasonableness imposed by civilization.

Although he emphasizes the intention or purpose of jokes, Freud cannot quite leave out of consideration his idea of energy discharge. For, in permitting the expression of suppressed or repressed impulses, jokes provide a yield of pleasure to the teller by draining the amount of energy required for maintaining defenses against these impulses. The listener (an essential person for a joke) presumably also obtains a similar yield of pleasure for the same reason.

To refer to a listener is to emphasize the social nature of the joke, and Freud is explicit on this point. Jokes may receive their formal structure and some of their content from the unconscious. But, unlike dreams, they are not compromise formations. Jokes do not violate the "condition of intelligibility," which is required if they are to be understood by a third person. They are, as Freud says, "the most social of all the mental functions that aim at a yield of pleasure" (179).

In view of Freud's emphasis on a joke's social nature and on the formal verbal constructions involved in the yield of pleasure, both E. H. Gombrich and Norman O. Brown have read Freud's book on jokes as his most important treatise on aesthetics. Replace wit with art, they suggest, and we have a provisional aesthetic theory.[23] Brown, in fact, argues that the view of art derived from *Jokes and their Relation to the Unconscious*—"art as pleasure, art as play, art as the recovery of childhood, art as making conscious the unconscious, art as a mode of instinctual liberation, art as the fellowship of men struggling for instinctual liberation"—places Freud squarely in the tradition of the romantic rejection of nineteenth-century science (Brown, 65–66). This is a provocative view, and it is partially confirmed by Freud's uncertainty in *Civilization and Its Discontents* as to whether the instinctual renunciation demanded by civilization is worth the price. But, finally, he says, it is, marginally, because the alternative is even worse—the return of a Hobbesian state of nature in which life is nasty, brutish, and short and thus even worse than in civilization. Peter Gay is surely closer to the essential Freud in his view of him as "the last of the philosophes"—a true heir of the Enlightenment who bases his hope for humankind on science and an acceptance of reality (Gay 1987, 41).[24]

The Theory of Sexuality

Three Essays on the Theory of Sexuality (1905) stands with *The Interpretation of Dreams* as one of the two most important works of Freud. Indeed, it completes *The Interpretation of Dreams* in an essential way by identifying and giving specific content to the instinctual energies behind those repressed infantile sexual wishes that "provide the most frequent and strongest motive-forces for the construction of dreams" (*SE,* 5:682). Like *The Interpretation of Dreams, Three Essays* was expanded and altered in the six editions that appeared over the next 20 years. A number of basic ideas—the sexual researches of children, the pregenital phases of development, and the libido theory—were added as late as 1915.

According to Strachey, Freud probably had the main lines of his theory of sexuality formulated by 1901 (*SE,* 7:129). He points to Freud's letters to Fliess of 3 and 15 October 1897 (during his self-analysis) as leading inevitably to the idea that sexual impulses in children occurred normally. These letters, of course, come after the letter in which he explains his reasons for doubting the seduction theory, and it is taken for granted that without the seduction theory he was almost compelled to hypothesize infantile sexuality. This is probably true, but it is interesting to see him writing on 6 December 1896 (when he still held the seduction theory) that behind the experience of seduction "lies the idea of abandoned *erotogenic zones*" (*Freud-Fliess,* 212; Freud's italics). Would Freud have added a theory of infantile sexuality to the seduction theory had he not abandoned it?

Although short, *Three Essays* is a complex, elegantly argued work. Here I try to do justice only to its central ideas. I begin with instinct theory.[25] An instinct, Freud says, is provisionally to be understood as the "psychical representative of an endosomatic, continuously flowing source of stimulation, as contrasted with a 'stimulus,' which is set up by *single* excitations coming from *without*" (*SE,* 7:168; Freud's italics). This definition, written in 1915 in one of Freud's many revisions of *Three Essays,* is contemporary with a slightly different one in the 1915 essay "Instincts and Their Vicissitudes": an instinct from a biological point of view "appears to us as a concept on the frontier between the mental and the somatic" and is the "psychical representative of the stimuli originating from within the organism and reaching the mind, as a measure of the demand made upon the mind for work in consequence of its connection with the body" (*SE,* 14:121–22). The source of these stimuli is a "process of excitation occurring in an organ," and the "immediate aim of the instinct lies in the removal of this organic stimulus" (*SE,* 7:168). Removal means discharge, and the mind that stimuli reach is the passive central nervous system, not the seemingly active mind that constructs dreams in *The Interpretation of Dreams.* Freud's intellectual debt to Brücke and to his own *Project* now makes an appearance at the heart of psychoanalytic theory.

I have already discussed the evidence against the brain's inability to generate its own activity. I must now mention some contemporary views on Freud's concept of instinct, which, as mentioned previously, became one of the touchstones of psychoanalytic orthodoxy. First, as Bucci says, energy (instinct) theory has "never been systematically formulated as a coherent hypothesis concerning the functions of a psychological—not a physiological—system." Such concepts as instinct, libido, cathexis, and hypercathexis have not been systematically defined and measured and "there is no longer any expectation that they can be" (Bucci, 22–23). Because of this lack of operational definition and confirmation (or disconfirmation), many psychoanalysts have called for a rejection of the concept of instinct. Second, Robert Holt and others have argued that Freud's view of instinct is based on the idea that a fixed amount of energy flows in a closed system. But living organisms are not closed systems; they are open systems that seek to maintain a steady state (Holt, 134). Third, Morris Eagle observes that sexuality is more interactional or relational than Freud's view of internally accumulating energy recognizes. The sexual tendencies (even more than hunger and thirst, and in animals as well as humans) depend on external stimuli for arousal. They do not exist as a continuous state of undischarged tension. And fourth, as Eagle also observes, the study of infants shows that they are stimulus-seeking organisms and that their "selective preferences for certain stimulus configurations are autonomous, inborn, natural propensities which appear at birth or shortly after birth."[26] This behavior is self-motivated, not caused by a need for discharge.

These are serious critiques of one of Freud's core ideas. Drives, after all, are motivation, so what is at issue is a theory of human motivation. What is being questioned in these four points is not Freud's search for motivational factors but the framing of his conclusions in a drive reduction model (based on the constancy principle) that does not receive support from research in biology and psychology. As writers like Bucci, Holt, Eagle, and many others (including many psychoanalysts) have recognized, the constancy principle and the drive/discharge theory are not at present scientifically tenable. Much of the history of psychoanalysis in the last 50 years has been an attempt to come to terms with problems associated with Freud's instinct theory.[27]

In *Three Essays* Freud is primarily concerned with the sexual instinct, which he bases on the biological idea of a basic need like hunger and which he calls libido. And he announces on the opening page that his view of libido will not be the one generally understood—that is, absent in childhood, beginning at puberty, related to the attraction between the sexes, and aimed at genital sexual union. This view, he says, contains a "number of errors, inaccuracies and hasty conclusions" (*SE,* 7:135).

A first error is that sexuality involves attraction between the sexes. The case of inversion (his word for homosexuality)—the attraction of men to men and women to women—forces him to conclude that no one is born fixed sexually to a particular object. Indeed, sexual aim and sexual object "are merely soldered together—a fact which we have been in danger of overlooking in consequence of the uniformity of the normal picture" (148). For Freud, "numerous deviations" occur in both the sexual object, which means the person from whom sexual attraction proceeds, and the sexual aim, which is the "act towards which the instinct tends" (135–36). As for the normal sexual aim as the union of the genitals in sexual intercourse, that too is brought into serious question by the perversions. Under the term "perversion," Freud includes mouth-to-genital contact (but not mouth to mouth); sexual use of the anal orifice; fetishism; voyeurism and exhibitionism (looking and being looked at); and sadism and masochism. Voyeurism/exhibitionism and sadism/masochism, he observes, occur regularly as paired opposites—that is, each has an active and a passive mode.

Why is Freud interested in perversion? The answer is clear: because analysis of the symptoms of adult neurotics (especially hysterics) shows that these symptoms represent instincts that would have to be described as perverse "if they could be expressed directly in phantasy and action without being diverted from consciousness" (165). All neurotics unconsciously show impulses directed to persons of their own sex (bisexuality), tendencies to the widest possible anatomical extension of sexual activity, and tendencies toward voyeurism/exhibitionism and sadism/masochism (166). What is lived out in perversions is repressed in neurotics. Thus, as Freud says in a famous formula, "*neuroses are, so to say, the negative of perversions*" (165; Freud's italics). How are these unconscious trends discovered? Through an analysis of the fantasy life of neurotics—among them the primal fantasies of overhearing one's parents make love, of having been seduced early in life, and of being threatened with castration—behind which lies the child's sexual life (226).

Thus Freud not only extends the definition of what is sexual far beyond its adult genital meaning. He also extends sexuality back to the beginning of life—yet another error corrected. His argument for infantile sexuality is entirely by analogy. Perversions are unarguably sexual even though their aim and object do not coincide with so-called normal sexuality. Neurotics show the same perverse sexual impulses, albeit repressed, in fantasies and symptoms, and many fantasies point to very early life. There must, then, be infantile sexuality. Almost from the beginning, Jung argued that Freud's adult patients were sexualizing their childhood experience retrospectively. Brian Farrell makes very much the same point. When Freud uncovers a history of masturbation in childhood, he mistakenly assumes that, because an adult's interest is sexual, the child's interest in the penis must be sexual also, and this, Farrell concludes, is a "whopping mistake." For Farrell, it is more appropriate to say that for the child this is preparatory activity—"activity which serves infantile functions and is preparatory to the later adult sexuality of the individual."[28] But if it's preparatory to adult sexuality, it seems reasonable to call it preparatory sexual activity, which is what Freud would certainly say. What is sexual now, he insists, is sexual in childhood. This is a perfectly plausible analogy, but it is not evidence of the actual content of the childhood experience. What, in fact, could constitute such evidence? In addition to the fantasies of neurotics, one answer for Freud is dreams—his own and those of his patients—many of which express sexual wishes toward one of the dreamer's parents. Another is the sexual theories of children, which he takes as reflecting their own sexual endowment. He later adds the direct observation of children (of whom Little Hans was the first) and the erotic nature of the transference as further support for the idea of infantile sexuality, which remains for him one of the core ideas of psychoanalysis. For many, the idea remains at best an unproven hypothesis, for others a mistake.

Having extended the concept of what is sexual and identified infantile sexuality, Freud now wants to understand how human sexuality develops. That it does develop is itself another corrected error. For Freud, we are not born with a sexual essence that simply appears at puberty. Our sexuality, whatever it becomes (perverse, heterosexual, homosexual) is the outcome of a long developmental process in which component instincts become more and more convergent. We are all born with the same polymorphously perverse (that is, capable of diffuse sexual pleasure from the whole body) disposition. From this point of view, the "exclusive sexual interest felt by men for women is also a problem that needs elucidating and is not a self-evident fact based upon an attraction that is ultimately of a chemical nature" (146 n). In short, we are not born with an essential sexuality of any kind, including a genital sexuality that at the appropriate time will subserve a reproductive function.

Component instincts are infantile sexual urges that are disconnected from each other and that achieve satisfaction either from the stimulation of specific erotogenic zones or from looking and being looked at and active and passive cruelty (his word). Some component instincts require erotogenic zones; others find pleasure in a more general way. But all are aspects of libido, which is the manifestation of the sexual instinct in the psyche. There are two pregenital stages of organization of the component instincts: an oral one with the oral (mouth and buccal mucosa) zone in the leading part; and an anal sadistic one where the component instinct of sadism is predominant and where the difference between the sexes lies in the contrast between active and passive impulses (197–99). An erotogenic zone, then, is in each case associated with a biological function that has survival value—in the oral stage, with nourishment; in the anal stage, with excretion. But for Freud the taking of nourishment is separable from the nonnourishing thumb sucking (sensual sucking) observed in the newborn. Sucking at the breast thus serves a dual purpose: the taking of nourishment and the satisfaction of oral sexuality. Oral gratification then continues in sensual sucking and the wishful fantasies (whatever their content) accompanying it. So Freud sees human sexuality from the beginning as detached from reality and hence especially prone to the wishful fantasizing of the primary process.

The final stage occurs when most of the component instincts come under the primacy of the genitals (which is not complete until puberty).[29] The genital stage (from age three to five) coincides with the sexual researches of childhood, is succeeded by a period of latency until puberty, and is then resumed in the sexual concerns of adolescence.[30] Only at this time does sexuality become subordinated to reproduction. Thus, for Freud, libido develops diphasically—in the psychosexual stages of early childhood and at puberty. A threefold result of this development is possible. First, normal sexuality develops if the component instincts are repressed and subordinated to the primacy of the genitals. In this case the component instincts continue to find a normal outlet in sexual foreplay, which involves a stimulation of nongenital erotogenic zones. Second, perversion occurs if the component instincts remain overpowering and compulsive. And third, neurosis occurs if there is excessive repression of infantile sexuality. In normality and neurosis, infantile sexuality is repressed and an amnesia for the childhood years results. In all three cases much of an adult's character is formed as a result of sexual excitations and by the ways in which a person attempts to hold such impulses in check. Sublimation may transform a sexual impulse into a nonsexual purpose and lead to cultural achievement of one kind or another (artistic creativity, say). Reaction formation, by turning an infantile impulse into its opposite, produces many adult character types (178).[31] Finally, it is important to understand that the development from oral to genital sexuality is never complete. A portion of libido always remains attached to each of the psychosexual stages. Freud calls this attachment a fixation, which he views as essential in the development of neurosis (242–43).

For Freud, the development of the libido begins in autoerotism—that is, sexual satisfaction is obtained from the child's own body. How, then, does autoerotism become object (the psychoanalytic term for person) relations? How does the human infant find an object? For Freud, the prototype of all object relations is the infant sucking at the mother's breast. But at first the mother's breast is not an object because there is as yet no conception of inner and outer for the infant. The breast becomes an object only as the infant perceives its absence and for which the infant substitutes its thumb. The first object is thus the lost breast, which will eventually become the person of the mother who first provides both nourishment and sexual satisfaction (181–82, 222). The infant, in short, finds an object in the person who initially satisfies its instinctual needs. Later, the child models its relations with other people on its relations as a suckling to its nursing mother. Thus, a child's "intercourse with anyone responsible for his care affords him an unending source of sexual excitation and satisfaction from his erotogenic zones" (222–23).

Later statements by Freud continue the idea of the mother as the first sexual object. For example, in "Analysis of a Phobia in a Five-Year-Old Boy" (1909), he says that Little Hans obtained "pleasure from his erotogenic zones with the help of the person who had looked after him—his mother, in fact: and thus the pleasure already pointed the way to object-choice" (*SE,* 10:108). And in "On Narcissism: An Introduction" (1914), he says that infants derive "their sexual objects from their experiences of satisfaction" (*SE,* 14:87). Eagle correctly observes that the logic of Freud's instinct theory explains the "child's attachment to mother in terms of the latter's role in providing instinctual gratifications" (Eagle, 9).[32] He argues, as do Greenberg and Mitchell, that this theory requires attachment to be a secondary, not a primary, mode (Greenberg and Mitchell, 21–49). Yet, as he says, the evidence of research on human and infrahuman behavior "overwhelmingly supports the idea of a primary and autonomous attachment instinctual system relatively independent of the hunger drive and of sex and aggression" (Eagle, 13). Here is yet another theoretical difficulty for contemporary psychoanalysts. In fact, long before the research to which Eagle refers, many psychoanalysts were already questioning the adequacy of drive theory to explain attachment or object relations. Answers to this questioning are diverse. Some involve combinations of drive theory with an object relational or attachment theory; others reject drive theory altogether and replace it with a purely relational paradigm.[33]

On Neurosis

Freud never wrote the big book on the neuroses that he mentions to Fliess (*Freud-Fliess,* 219). There is thus no equivalent for the neuroses to the comprehensive works on dreams, parapraxes, and jokes. But there is enough material from which to determine Freud's approach after 1900 to the cause, structure, and treatment of neurosis.

In terms of cause there is a basic continuity between his views before and after 1900. He still sees the sexual life of human beings as the necessary cause of neurosis. But "sexual" now means the widened view of sexuality presented in *Three Essays.* As he says in "My Views on the Part Played by Sexuality in the Aetiology of the Neuroses," however much his views have altered since the abandonment of the seduction theory, sexuality and the infantile have been constant. Infantile sexual trauma has become the infantilism of sexuality (*SE,* 7:275). This change does not alter the fact that the essence of neurosis "lies in disturbances of the sexual processes, the processes which determine in the organism the formation and utilization of sexual libido" (278). The major difference between the idea of sexual seduction and infantile sexuality is that now fantasies of seduction (and other postpubertal fantasies) are regarded as disguised memories of the patient's own infantile sexual activity. Fantasies are thus inserted between the "childish impressions" and the symptoms of the neurosis (274).

A number of consequences follow from this change. First, accidental influences (seduction and other traumatic events) recede in importance and "factors of constitution and heredity" increase in importance, where by "heredity" Freud means sexual constitution and not a hereditary tendency to nervous disease (275–76). With his new emphasis on heredity, Freud begins to rethink his original concept of defense as the expelling from consciousness of incompatible ideas (some of which are sexual), which find their way back to consciousness and create symptoms. The concepts of infantile sexuality and the development of the libido compel Freud to conclude that what is repressed is an instinctual impulse—or, more precisely, the mental representation (fantasies) of these impulses. Some of these fantasies seem to be perverse. They arise from erotogenic zones (oral and anal) that, "in view of the direction of the subject's development, can only arouse unpleasurable feelings" (178). Consequently, Freud says, they are repressed. So, for example, anal erotism—the pleasure of retaining, expelling, or playing with feces—because it is "unserviceable for sexual aims" in our present civilization, falls victim to shame, disgust, and morality (*SE,* 9:171). The same fate, of course, awaits the boy's sexual attachment to his mother during the phallic stage. But *repressed* doesn't mean "gone" or "inactive."

Freud's major work on repression is a 1915 essay entitled "Repression." In this paper repression occurs in three phases, the first of which is primal repression, which occurs in early childhood and accounts for the amnesia for infantile sexuality. In primal repression an ideational representative of an instinct is "denied entrance into the conscious." The result is fixation—the "representative in question persists unaltered from then onwards and the instinct remains attached to it" (*SE,* 14:148). It exists in the unconscious and is subject to the characteristics of the unconscious—the pleasure principle (pressure for tension reduction), the primary process (unbound and mobile energy), exemption from mutual contradiction, timelessness, and the priority of psychical over external reality.[34] Cut off from contact with reality, these repressed impulses (oral, anal, and phallic) do not undergo the corrective development of the reality principle. Thus, the content of the unconscious, Freud says in "The Unconscious," "may be compared with an aboriginal population in the mind" (195). This population, moreover, has no language. In consciousness an object is presented by word and thing. An unconscious presentation "is the presentation of the thing alone. The system *Ucs.* contains the thing-cathexes of the objects, the first and true object-cathexes: the system *Pcs.* comes about by this thing-presentation being hypercathected through being linked with the word-presentations corresponding to it" (201–2). Repression, in short, denies a thing-presentation a translation into words. The primally repressed unconscious—the infantile core of the unconscious for Freud—cannot be observed directly and appears in consciousness only indirectly in dreams and neurotic symptoms and to some extent in parapraxes and jokes.

The second phase is repression proper, which, in late childhood, adolescence, and thereafter, affects mental derivatives of the repressed instinct or trains of thought that have become associatively connected to these mental derivatives. To some extent these ideas are repressed from the direction of consciousness, but equally important is the attraction exerted on them by primarily repressed instinctual representations.

Probably, Freud concludes, repression proper occurs because of a cooperation between conscious and primally repressed forces—that is, "repression would fail in its purpose if these two forces did not cooperate, if there were not something previously repressed ready to receive what is repelled by the conscious" (148). The third phase of repression is the return of the repressed, which signals the failure of repression and the appearance of neurotic symptoms (154).

To illustrate these aspects of repression, I return to the case of Miss Lucy R. Lucy's presenting symptom—the smell of burnt pudding—signifies the return of the repressed, while the conflict between her ego and her love for her employer shows that repression is operative. But this conflict is not an infantile one, so the repression must be repression proper. Had Freud reviewed this case 10 years later, he certainly would have concluded that his original analysis was superficial. Now, he would require evidence of primal repression—Lucy's already repressed infantile love for her father, say—with which her adult conflict can be associatedly connected. After 1900, only this connection of repression proper to primal repression satisfies Freud as a full psychoanalytic interpretation. Anything less lacks the dimension of depth.

What is the conscious force that cooperates with primal repression to produce repression proper? And how does primal repression occur? Not until 1910 does Freud turn to this question. Then, in "The Psycho-Analytic View of Psychogenic Disturbance of Vision," he identifies the ego instinct (the first use of this term) and emphasizes that a "quite specially important part" is played by the opposition between the sexual and the ego instincts. The ego, he says, "feels threatened by the claims of the sexual instincts and fends them off by repressions" (*SE,* 11:214–15). Here repression clearly originates with the ego, which as the self-preservative instinct is oriented toward reality. Wollheim observes that Freud does not say whether he means that the ego instincts are involved in primal repression or repression proper, which does indeed add confusion to an already complex subject (Wollheim, 162). In "Repression" Freud refers to the anticathectic energy with which the system Pcs. "protects itself from the pressure upon it of the unconscious idea." This is the "permanent expenditure" of energy in primal repression; anticathexis is thus the "sole mechanism of primal repression" (*SE,* 14:181). The system Pcs. is the topographical domain of the ego instinct, so I take it that Freud means that the ego is involved in both primal repression and repression proper. Freud repeatedly denies that repression occurs as the result of a conflict between opposing sexual trends (as, presumably, it would in primal repression without ego involvement). Otherwise, those critics who claim that psychoanalysis is pansexual would be right, and Freud repeatedly denies this charge.[35] He insists that conflict arises between the sexual and the nonsexual instincts and that it is this conflict that produces neurosis. Like dreams, neuroses are compromise formations, and the symptoms of neuroses represent both the sexual life of the patient and the repressive activity of the ego.[36]

But this conflict, though a necessary cause, is not a sufficient cause for neurosis. All human beings arrive at puberty with more or less the same conflicted sexual constitution. Yet not all human beings become neurotic. For one thing, there are accidental experiences in childhood that may awaken or inhibit an individual's sexual disposition (*SE,* 16:361). But beyond these accidental experiences of childhood, Freud also describes precipitating factors that affect adults and that for some adults lead to neurosis.

In "Types of Onset of Neurosis" (1910) he describes four such precipitating causes. The first is external frustration. When a person's need for love is satisfied by a real external object he or she is healthy; when that object is withdrawn without a substitute the person becomes neurotic. The second cause is an attempt to adapt to external reality that fails because of internal factors of disposition and infantile experience. Again the result is frustration, in this case of an inner need. The third cause involves an inhibition of development—the libido never leaves its infantile fixations. Here disposition is the predominant cause of neurosis. (Freud admits that this third cause appears to be an exaggeration of the second.) Finally, there is the effect of the period of life (puberty or menopause) with its concomitant increase of the quantity of libido, which leads to a relative frustration because of the incapacity of the external world to grant satisfaction to this increased quantity. In each of these four cases (which are rarely seen in pure form) frustration and a consequent damming up of libido (a familiar idea from the actual neuroses) are the constants (*SE,* 12:231–38).

Neurosis, then, is the result of a complex and variable interaction between accidental and constitutional elements—between endowment (sexual disposition) and chance, as Freud likes to say (99). Indeed, the complexity and variability in the interaction between accident and endowment—those two extremes in the complemental series—make it impossible to predict who will fall ill and who will not. Like history and evolutionary theory, psychoanalysis can only construct the most likely story about the past.

Given the complexity of this etiological situation, what, then, is the path to symptom formation? People fall ill with neurosis, Freud says, because of frustration, because "reality prevents them from satisfying their sexual wishes" (*SE,* 16:300). Some people, of course, can tolerate such frustration without falling ill. Further, the sexual instincts are extremely plastic—one can take the place of the other, or they can change their object for one more easily attainable. Then there is sublimation, in which a sexual trend is replaced by a social aim. Still, Freud argues, there is a "limit to the amount of unsatisfied libido that human beings on the average can put up with" (345–46). Anyone, therefore, is liable to libidinal frustration (that is, the accumulation of a quantity of undischarged instinctual energy) beyond his or her capacity for abstinence.

But for pathology to occur an internal frustration must be added to an external one. The external frustration removes one way of satisfaction; the internal frustration attempts to prevent an alternative mode of satisfaction, and this is the point around which neurotic conflict appears. For external frustration turns the libido inward and sets it on a retrogressive path to an earlier stage of libidinal development where satisfaction was once achieved. This is the same process of regression by which dreams are formed. Regression is a "return of the libido to earlier stopping-places in its development"—that is, to stages of fixation established by primal repression (342). It is a twofold process: a temporal one insofar as libido moves "back to stages of development that are earlier in time," and a formal one in that "original and primitive methods of psychical expression" (that is, primary process) are employed in manifesting need (*SE,* 11:49). To move from secondary to primary process is to substitute wish and fantasy for reality—which is for Freud precisely the case in neurosis. Moreover, regression may involve a return to the first objects of the libido, the now prohibited parents (as in hysteria) or a return to an earlier sexual organization (as in the anal sadistic organization of obsessional neurosis). In both object and organizational regression, repression (both primal and repression proper) has now rendered the search for internal satisfaction not pleasurable but unpleasurable. Regression without repression would lead to perversion, not neurosis (*SE,* 16:343–44). As Freud says, the "theory of repression is the cornerstone on which the whole structure of psycho-analysis rests" (*SE,* 14:16).

From this point of regression on, the three major psychoneuroses (or transference neuroses, as Freud begins to call them in this period) diverge in their paths to symptom formation. In "Repression" Freud gives a very compressed but useful short account of the divergences among hysteria, anxiety neurosis (phobia), and obsessional neurosis. In hysteria the "ideational content of the instinctual representative" (that is, of the infantile fantasy or memory cathected by the regressed libido) is completely repressed, while the "quota of affect" attached to that representative is converted into a sensory or motor symptom. The symptom is a substitutive (or compromise) formation that represents both the return of the repressed and the resistance of the ego to that return. Because hysteria makes use of external substitution in the form of numerous symptoms, the attempt at repression is not successful. But in terms of suppressing affect it is often totally successful because the symptoms bind the anxiety (*SE,* 14:155–56). Dora, the 18-year-old patient in "Fragment of an Analysis of a Case of Hysteria" (1905), is not so fortunate for, in addition to such symptoms as a nervous cough, aphonia, dyspnea, and unilateral headaches, she also had periods of depression and was unsociable. For Freud, Dora's physical symptoms are "nothing else than *the patient's sexual activity*" (*SE,* 7:115; Freud's italics), which on analysis includes a repressed love for a friend of her father's, repressed incestuous love for her father, and repressed lesbian feelings for a female friend who was also having an affair with Dora's father.[37]

In phobias the substitutive formation occurs by a process of displacement. A father is loved and feared simultaneously. After repression the father is no longer an object of libido, but a substitute—an animal, say—now replaces him. There appears the fear of an animal rather than a demand for love from the father. The result is a phobia (*SE,* 14:155). In "Analysis of a Phobia in a Five-Year-Old Boy," Freud sees Hans's fear of horses biting him as a displaced fear of his father whose anger he feared because of his erotic longings for his mother. But the phobic animal in this case is overdetermined (as, for Freud, most symptoms, like images in dreams, are). The horse is also Hans's mother and sister. Here the association is not to biting horses but to horses that fall down and get hurt or die. The falling horse, as Freud shows, is the dying father (dying because Hans wishes him dead), the mother in childbirth, and the new sister whose presence Hans resents and whom he wishes his mother might drop while bathing her (*SE,* 10:128). For Freud, repression in phobias is "radically unsuccessful" because all it does is replace the idea or object; unpleasure in the form of anxiety (Hans fears even going out) remains (*SE,* 14:155).[38]

Finally, there are obsessional neuroses. Obsessional illness arises when a hostile impulse against a loved one is repressed. At first, repression is wholly successful, as the hostile impulse disappears and a substitute in the form of conscientiousness (for Freud, not a symptom) appears. The mechanism here Freud calls reaction formation, which means that a feeling of increased love replaces the repressed hate. But this repression cannot hold, the hostile affect returns as "social anxiety, moral anxiety and unlimited self-reproaches," and the rejected idea is "replaced by a *substitute by displacement,* often a displacement on to something very small or indifferent" (157; Freud's italics). In the 29-year-old lawyer Ernst Lanzer (better known as the Rat Man because of his story of an Eastern punishment involving rats and also because of his associations to the word "rat") Freud found an exemplary obsessive. "Notes upon a Case of Obsessional Neurosis" (1909) portrays Lanzer's one-year analysis and cure (only to die in World War I). He presented with the usual confusing symptoms of obsession compulsion—a fear that something might happen to his father (who had been dead for nine years) and the lady he loved, compulsive impulses (such as cutting his throat with a razor), and prohibitions on what he could do (*SE,* 10:158). Freud sees the core of the Rat Man's illness in his ambivalent love and hate toward his father—an ambivalence that carries over to other relationships, such as that with the lady he loves. This hatred, of course, is repressed and appears as doubt and self-reproaches about almost anything he does or doesn't do. The love is intensified as his oversolicitous concern about something happening to his father or his lady, a concern that for Freud betrays the hostile repressed wish.[39]

Neurosis is an inexhaustible subject in Freud's work, just as Freud's interest in it is inexhaustible. It is, after all, the core material of psychoanalysis. I have tried to present only a very general overview of Freud's theory of the cause and structure of neurosis from 1900 to 1913. I will make only one other point and then move on to other (but related) material. The point is Freud's discussion of what the ego gets out of neurosis. In addressing this strange idea, Freud distinguishes between primary and secondary advantages. A primary gain for the ego is an internal advantage because falling ill saves much psychic effort. A flight into illness may be the best response to internal conflict—though only at first. A secondary advantage is always external—that is, it is motivated by a desire to control or manipulate people (as when a child falls ill to compel parental attention away from siblings). Such primary and secondary advantages are not the essential causes of neuroses. But they must be recognized, Freud says, as an element of the resistance of symptoms to treatment (*SE,* 7:43, 16:382–85).

The Oedipus Complex

For an idea that for many people is one of the basic Freudian concepts, the Oedipus complex evolves very slowly to its central place in Freud's thinking. True, he reports Oedipal dreams and refers to Sophocles' *Oedipus Rex* in *The Interpretation of Dreams.* The three case studies of this period—Dora, Little Hans, and the Rat Man—illustrate Oedipal dynamics: Dora's repressed love for her father; Hans's love for his mother and rivalry with (but love for) his father; and the Rat Man's ambivalent feelings for the father who stands between him and the sensual gratification he desires.[40] In Dora's case Freud alludes to the legend of Oedipus at one point. He refers to Hans as a little Oedipus. And with the Rat Man he refers to a complex that deserves to be called the "*nuclear complex of the neuroses,*" which must mean the Oedipus complex (*SE,* 10:208 n; Freud's italics).[41] So the dynamics of the cases are Oedipal, but the concept remains unnamed.

In *Five Lectures on Psycho-Analysis* (1909) Freud writes again of the nuclear (or incest) complex of the neuroses and connects it with the story of King Oedipus (*SE,* 11:47). But only in 1910 in "A Special Type of Choice of Object Made by Men" does he refer explicitly to the Oedipus complex (171). In this essay the Oedipus complex is defined as a desire for the mother and a hatred of the father.[42] Though no further reference to Oedipus occurs until 1913, Freud does explore the relationship of the boy to both father and mother in "Leonardo da Vinci and a Memory of His Childhood" and of a boy to his father in the Schreber case (in 1910 and 1911).[43] We can see Freud gradually coming to the conclusion that regression to or fixation at the developmental stage of Oedipal object choice is bound to lead to neurosis. It frustrates the need for the young man or woman to move away from parental to new object relations in adolescence and thereafter. In addition, such regression or fixation leads to an internal conflict between an unconscious incestuous object choice and a conscious repudiation of that choice.[44] In an adult man a continuing libidinal attachment to the mother may inhibit the changing of sensual longing into impulses of affection; the man may then be left with a division between the affectionate and the sensual components of love and so be unable to unite these currents into the love of one woman.[45] Freud believes, further, that even children can experience Oedipal conflict and become neurotic—as in the cases of Hans and the Rat Man, whom Freud believes to have been obsessional from the age of four or five on. Indeed, he came to think of childhood neurosis as the rule, not the exception. In his final word on the subject in the unfinished *An Outline of Psycho-Analysis* (1940), he says that "neuroses are acquired only in early childhood (up to the age of six)" and that in "every case the later neurotic illness links up with the prelude in childhood" (*SE,* 23:184). As for choice of neurosis—the predisposition to become a hysteric, an obsessive, a paranoid, or a schizophrenic—that too is established in childhood by a fixation in one of the stages of libidinal development—for the transference neuroses, in the Oedipal stage (*SE,* 12:317–26). The task of detaching from the parents (and hence from this Oedipal fixation) is "set to everyone." But neurotics, Freud says, arrive at no solution to the Oedipus complex, and so the "son remains all his life beneath his father's authority and he is unable to transfer his libido to an outside sexual object." The same is true for the daughter, except that the relationship is "changed round" (*SE,* 16:337).

By 1909 or 1910, then, the Oedipus complex had become the nuclear complex of the neuroses. In 1913 Freud published *Totem and Taboo: Some Points of Agreement between the Mental Lives of Savages and Neurotics,* in which the Oedipus complex is not only the nuclear complex of the neuroses but also the beginning of religion, morals, society, and art. This book is not Freud's first venture in applying psychoanalysis to the study of a cultural phenomenon. In "Obsessive Actions and Religious Practices" (1907) he had already pointed to similarities between obsessive and religious rituals (*SE,* 9:117–27). But the scope of this earlier essay pales by comparison to the aim of *Totem and Taboo.* Freud wants to accomplish nothing less than an explanation of the origin of civilization. Though sometimes ambivalent about the book (he once referred to it as a scientific myth and on one occasion thought that a British critic's description of it as a just-so story was a good joke), Freud never abandoned his basic ideas and, indeed, continued to restate and develop them—as in *Moses and Monotheism* (1939).

In the first chapter of *Totem and Taboo,* "The Horror of Incest," Freud surveys the incest taboo among the aborigines of Australia, the Melanesians, the Bantu, and others. The horror of incest of these people, he notes, is in striking agreement with the "mental life of neurotic patients" (*SE,* 13:17). Freud wants to establish that the taboo on incest exists because human beings have a propensity to break the taboo. So he cites approvingly James Frazer's (1854–1941) critique of Edward Westermarck's (1862–1939) thesis of the natural aversion to incest. A law is not needed, Frazer says, where there is no tendency to violate it.[46] In chapter 2 Freud studies the ambivalence of people who obey taboos and concludes that the "basis of taboo is a prohibited action, for performing which a strong inclination exists in the unconscious" (32). There is a strong similarity, he argues, between "taboo usages" and obsessive ceremonials (28). In chapter 3 he turns to a consideration of animism, magic, and the omnipotence of thoughts. Animism (the peopling of the world with spirits "both benevolent and malignant") is a complete worldview that precedes the religious and scientific worldviews (76–77). Magic, he thinks, is an "animistic technique" for dealing with spirits (78). The belief that through magic spirits can be mastered Freud calls "omnipotence of thoughts" (a phrase used by the Rat Man), which is characteristic of neurotics (85). Like neurotics, people at the animistic stage think themselves capable of controlling the external world through the magic of their wishes. Animism is thus a psychological, not a speculative or scientific, system, and it constitutes one of the points of agreement between savages and neurotics.

In the fourth chapter Freud returns to totemism, which he has already introduced in chapter 1. Drawing largely on Frazer's *Totemism and Exogamy* (1910), he follows Frazer in defining totemism as a religious and social system (a totem clan) whose members are brothers and sisters "bound to help and protect one another" (105). Freud identifies two basic elements of the totemic organization, both taboos: first, the totem animal (originally, he says, all totems were animals and were regarded as ancestors of the different clans) could not be killed; and second, members of the clan were forbidden to have sexual intercourse with each other (exogamy). Any adequate explanation of totemism, he says, must account for these two elements, and it should be "at once a historical and a psychological one" (107–8).

Freud's solution is both. Taking a clue from Darwin that humans, like the higher apes, originally lived in small groups or hordes ruled by a dominant male; from James Jasper Atkinson's (d. 1899) idea of a revolution in which the dominant male was killed and eaten; from William Robertson Smith (1846–1894) that a totem meal of a sacrificial animal formed a part of the totemic system; and from his own experience with phobia (Little Hans), Freud presents his theory of the primal horde. In the primal horde there is no totemism. There is only a "violent and jealous" father who keeps the females for himself and "drives away his sons as they grow up." But one day (actually many days over many years in numerous hordes) the sons, the brothers, banded together, "killed and devoured their father and so made an end of the patriarchal horde" (141). United, and with perhaps a new weapon, they succeeded together in what they could not do alone. In devouring the primal father, each brother identified with him and acquired some of his strength. Thus, Smith's totem meal is a "repetition and a commemoration of this memorable and criminal deed, which was the beginning of so many things—of social organization, of moral restrictions and of religion" (142).

For the sons both hated and loved their father, though where the love came from is mysterious. It originates, apparently, in the primal ambivalence of human beings, and this ambivalence remains a central idea for Freud in many future works. When the sons had satisfied their hate, they felt again their original affection for him. A sense of guilt now appeared, and the dead father became even stronger than he had been when alive. By forbidding the killing of the totem (the substitute for the father), the sons "revoked their deed." And they renounced its fruits "by resigning their claim to the women who had now been set free." The sense of guilt thus created the two fundamental taboos of totemism—the prohibition of parricide and of incest—"which for that very reason inevitably corresponded to the two repressed wishes of the Oedipus complex" (143).

There are several consequences of these events. First, all later religions must solve the problem of guilt for the crime from which civilization arose. Second, the nature of ambivalence leads not only to remorse but also to a remembrance of the victory over the father. In the sacrifice of the totem meal (the Christian Communion is a good example) the crime is repeated again and again. Third, the patriarchal horde is replaced by a fraternal clan, and so greatly influences the development of society (145–46). And finally, each newborn is forever sentenced to reliving the primal crime in the form of his (this is a male myth) Oedipus complex.

No one—certainly no anthropologist—believes this story.[47] The main reason for disbelief is the lack of empirical evidence that a primal horde as Freud describes it ever existed. Even if primate studies clearly indicated such a horde (which, as a nonprofessional in the field, I understand they do not unequivocally demonstrate), this would not prove that our own hominid ancestors lived in such a group. Nothing is more uncertain than paleoanthropology, where several million years are represented by only a few partial fossils.

But contemporary problems in constructing cultural history from fossil remains are only a part of the problem with Freud's *Totem and Taboo.* As Edwin Wallace shows in *Freud and Anthropology,* Freud bases his anthropological views on an evolutionary anthropology that was a legacy of the late nineteenth century and that was already, even as he wrote, being replaced by the functional anthropology that has dominated the field almost unchallenged to the present. To put the case as briefly as possible: first, Freud accepted the psychic unity of all the populations he discussed so that he was prepared to believe that the totem animal must symbolize the father for all of them; second, he equated contemporary "primitives" both with neurotics and with primal man; third, he repeated the evolutionists' doctrine of survivals by explaining the incest taboo to persons other than blood relations as a survival of a period of group marriage for which there is no evidence; fourth, he saw all cultures as evolving through the same stages from animistic to religious to scientific, which meant that the Western adult was at the mature end of a continuum that placed the primitive, the child, and the neurotic at its lower end.[48] As if this weren't criticism enough, Robert Paul points out that Freud's central analogy is untenable. A civilization, he argues, "just is *not* like a person. It does not have a childhood, a latency, an adolescence, or a maturity; it does not have a collective 'mind' or subjectivity, and it cannot in any meaningful way be understood as the sort of entity that could have a neurosis."[49]

So the theory of the primal horde and most of Freud's anthropological assumptions have by now been discarded. Yet the theory of the primal horde continues to fascinate. Paul himself, though highly critical of the dubious anthropology of *Totem and Taboo,* attempts to show in *Moses and Civilization* that the theory of the primal horde and Freud's later work on Moses is about an event that occurred, not in history, but in one of the shaping mythic narratives of Western culture. He then proceeds to argue that the Pentateuch is actually the story of the primal horde where Moses is the perpetrator of the primal crime against the pharaoh and the aftermath of that crime is the establishment of the Judeo-Christian tradition. For Paul, moreover, this tradition is precisely the obsessive, ritualistic one that Freud suggests in his analogy between obsessive and religious ritual. Paul Roazen, on the other hand, views Freud's just-so story as a version of the rationalist social contract theory of Western society where the brothers replaced the father with a body of rules.[50] Neither of these views treats Freud's story as literal.

A serious issue that emerges from the story of the primal horde is Freud's Lamarckianism. Jean-Baptiste Lamarck (1744–1829) published his *Zoological Philosophy* in 1809, the year of Darwin's birth, in which he proposed four laws of evolutionary change. The fourth is the law of the inheritance of acquired characteristics, which means that parents can transmit to the next generation features developed during their lifetime. In contemporary biology, this idea has been discarded. As Colin Tudge says, such a "mechanism could not operate unless information from the muscle cells could somehow be transmitted to the sperm or eggs."[51] This law is apparently invoked by Freud in *Totem and Taboo* when he says, in trying to explain how psychic processes continue from generation to generation, that a "part of the problem seems to be met by the inheritance of psychical dispositions which, however, need to be given some sort of impetus in the life of the individual before they can be roused into actual operation" (*SE,* 13:158). As a description of how a genetic endowment is activated by environmental stimuli, this is a perfectly accurate statement. The trouble is that the inheritance of psychical dispositions means the inheritance of acquired characteristics, which suggests that the primal crime is inherited by all subsequent generations—as Tudge says, a biological impossibility. So Freud's *Totem and Taboo* is usually described as Lamarckian even though this is the only sentence in the book that can be so construed and in spite of the fact that he immediately proceeds to describe a purely ontogenetic, not phylogenetic, explanation of the transmission of the primal crime. As he says, an "unconscious understanding" of the "customs, ceremonies and dogmas left behind by the original relation to the father may have made it possible for later generations to take over their heritage of emotion" (159). This is possible, presumably, because each generation experiences the same ambivalence as the original band of brothers—not because of the inheritance of the brother's ambivalence but because of a common human nature that necessarily reacts with love and hate toward the father's authority. The Lamarckianism of *Totem and Taboo* is greatly exaggerated.

Not, however, Freud's belief in the inheritance of acquired characteristics, even if that idea is restricted to one sentence in *Totem and Taboo.* But did Freud get the idea from Lamarck? Ritvo thinks not. She argues that he got the idea originally from Darwin, who was himself a Lamarckian on this one point. Darwin saw the idea of the inheritance of acquired characteristics (as transmitted by use or disuse of an organ or by habit) as sharing a role with natural selection in the transformation of species (Ritvo, 31–59, 64–73). Tudge thinks that Darwin was never really committed to this idea. Lacking an understanding of genetics, he needed it to explain how, once natural selection had produced an organism (say, a faster horse), that organism gave birth to offspring like itself (that is, faster horses) but also different. He needed, in other words, to explain both heredity and variety (Tudge, 89). In any case Freud would have found the idea of the inheritance of acquired characteristics in Darwin.[52]

But, as Ritvo shows, Freud also read Lamarck. In two letters of 1916 and some of his correspondence of 1917 and 1918, he does refer to Lamarck. Most of this correspondence is with Hungarian psychoanalyst Sándor Ferenczi (1873–1933) about a joint project on the relation of Lamarck to psychoanalysis. The project was never completed. But in 1983 Ilse Grubrich-Simitis, editor of the Freud-Ferenczi letters, discovered among Freud's letters to Ferenczi a draft of a lost paper that has since been published as *A Phylogenetic Fantasy: Overview of the Transference Neuroses.* The essay attempts to show that the dispositions to anxiety hysteria (phobia), conversion hysteria, and obsessional neurosis represent "regressions to phases that the whole human race had to go through at some time from the beginning to the end of the Ice Age, so that at that time all human beings were the way only some of them are now today, by virtue of their hereditary tendency and by means of new acquisition."[53] So neurotics today recapitulate a phylogenetic inheritance from this period, just as the Oedipus complex in each individual recapitulates the primal crime. This is Ernst Haeckel's (1834–1919) biogenetic law—ontogeny recapitulates phylogeny—to which Freud subscribed and which has been challenged by contemporary evolutionary theory.[54] For Freud, it is a crucial element of his belief in the inheritance of acquired characteristics.

Whatever its source (and I agree with Ritvo that he got nothing from Lamarck not already obtained from Darwin) Freud stresses the phylogenetic origin of neurosis, fantasies, and much of the content of normal peoples' experience in many works after 1916. Thus, in *Introductory Lectures on Psycho-Analysis* he says that "each individual somehow recapitulates in an abbreviated form the entire development of the human race, into phylogenetic prehistory too. . . . symbolic connections, which the individual has never acquired by learning, may justly claim to be regarded as a phylogenetic heritage" (*SE,* 15:199). Or again, from the Wolf Man case, Freud argues that, though threats of castration came from women, the Wolf Man had to turn his father into the terrifying castrator because he "had to fit into a phylogenetic pattern, and he did so, although his personal experiences may not have agreed with it" (*SE,* 17:86). Wherever, he continues later in the case, "experiences fail to fit in with the hereditary schema, they become remodelled in the imagination" (119). From this point of view, each of the primal fantasies—witnessing the parents in intercourse (primal scene), castration, and seduction—are phylogenetic holdovers. Finally, in *Group Psychology and the Analysis of the Ego* (1921) and *Moses and Monotheism* (1939), Freud uses the idea of the primal horde as a crucial element of his argument. In *Moses and Monotheism,* in fact, he abandons completely the idea from *Totem and Taboo* of tradition in the form of customs, ceremonies, and dogmas as the transmitter of the memory of the primal crime. Here he argues that a tradition survives, not by oral or written communication, but as a phylogenetic memory trace (*SE,* 23:99–101).

How deeply does Freud hold these ideas? Very deeply, apparently. When Jones asked him to alter a sentence in *Moses and Monotheism* that was too Lamarckian and that no biologist regarded as tenable, he was told by Freud that the biologists were wrong, the passage must stay, and that biological development was impossible for him to picture without this factor. "It is not easy," Jones says, "to account for the fixity with which Freud held this opinion and the determination with which he ignored all the biological evidence to the contrary" (Jones 1957, 3:313).

Most, if not all, psychoanalysts do not regard Freud's belief in the inheritance of acquired characteristics as either essential to or central in psychoanalysis. For them, the development of each individual during the prolonged childhood typical of humans is enough to account for the conflicts and ambivalence, as well as the general similarities, of human growth. They are content, therefore, to limit themselves to the ontogeny of development and, as Slavin and Kriegman say, to interpret Freud's phylogenetic speculations as an illustrative metaphor about the intrapsychic conflict observed in the individual (Slavin and Kriegman, 37).

Slavin and Kriegman agree that works such as *Totem and Taboo* and *Moses and Monotheism* are metaphorical, but not simply as illustrative of individual conflict. They argue that Freud's evolutionary thinking "can be understood as a search for what modern evolutionists . . . would call the 'social selection pressures' that shaped the intricate, inner design of the psyche" and that, for this purpose, he used one aspect of Larmarckian theory. For example, they read the following passage as referring to these social selection pressures: "There is naturally nothing to prevent our supposing that the instincts themselves are, at least in part, precipitates of the effects of external stimulation, which in the course of phylogenesis have brought about modifications in the living substance" (*SE,* 14:120). This sounds more like environmental stimuli in general rather than social pressures alone, but the point remains the same—endogenous drives can be traced back to the "shaping effects of ancient *external* (social) experiences."

Unfortunately, Slavin and Kriegman conclude, Freud lacked an understanding of the genetic base of natural selection (as did Darwin) as well as recent developments in the "evolutionary theory of mutuality and conflict in nature" (such as William Hamilton's concept of inclusive fitness or Robert Trivers's parent-offspring conflict theory) that make possible a more sophisticated "analysis of motivation in social creatures such as ourselves." Overall, then, "Freud was far from being in a position intellectually to apply evolutionary thinking in a very powerful, not to mention critical, way to the structure of psychoanalytic theory" (35, 40; Slavin and Kriegman's italics). What Freud could not do Slavin and Kriegman want contemporary psychoanalysts to do—use evolutionary theory to build a bridge between contemporary psychoanalytic theory and modern biology.[55]

One final question: does Freud believe in the primal crime as a historical fact? Is the Wolf Man's primal scene a real event or a fantasy constructed out of phylogenetic inheritance? Even obsessives, he says on the closing page of *Totem and Taboo,* who are punishing themselves for purely psychical events are also reflecting a historical reality. For in childhood they really had all the impulses that have now become an excessive morality. To establish the analogy between neurotics and primitive man more fully, he concludes, we must suppose that in the beginning psychical reality coincided with factual reality and that "primitive men actually *did* what all the evidence shows that they intended to do" (*SE,* 13:161; Freud's italics). Here, all these years after the seduction theory has been replaced by the primacy of psychic reality, is the old question: what reality, if any, lies behind the fantasy?

Chapter Four

New Directions (1914–1922)

The period now under consideration begins with Freud's most polemical work—*On the History of the Psycho-Analytic Movement.* The occasion for this tendentious book was the recent secession (his word) from the psychoanalytic movement of two of its most visible members—Alfred Adler (1870–1937) and Carl G. Jung (1875–1961). Freud was concerned that Adler's and Jung's ongoing work would be misconstrued as psychoanalysis by an unsuspecting public, and he wanted to set the record straight. In the book, he insists that he is in the best position to know what psychoanalysis is and how it differs from other ways of investigating the mind (*SE,* 14:7).

In 1900 there was no psychoanalytic movement. There was only Freud. By 1902 (the same year he received his long-delayed title of Professor) the situation began to change. In that year the Wednesday Society began to meet in Freud's study. The meetings were informal and small (at first only four others—among them Adler—besides Freud). The first four were all physicians, but over the years many nonmedical participants joined the group. An interest in psychoanalysis was the common bond. Each week one member of the group presented a paper; then after a break for refreshments the paper was discussed. Freud always had the last word.

By 1906 the group had 17 members. The members now decided to hire a secretary to record attendance and dues and take notes of each meeting.[1] The secretary was the young Otto Rank (1884–1939), who became a distinguished psychoanalyst in his own right. With larger numbers, Freud's study was too small, so the society rented a meeting hall. In 1908 the Wednesday Society became the Vienna Psychoanalytical Society. Freud complains in *On the History of the Psycho-Analytic Movement* about his difficulty in establishing friendly relations among the members and of the "disputes about priority" that continually broke out (*SE,* 14:25). He was pleased to have students, but his first Viennese followers were also exasperating him.

In 1907 Max Eitingen (1881–1943) arrived from Zurich—the first person from a foreign country to come to Freud to study psychoanalysis.

He came as an emissary from the Burghölzli Mental Hospital, where there was a lively interest in psychoanalysis. One of those interested was Jung, who was then the chief resident physician. The result of Eitingen's visit and of Freud's correspondence with Jung (to whom he first wrote in 1906) was the first international congress of psychoanalysis in 1908 in Salzburg.[2] In 1910 at the second international congress, Jung was elected (at Freud's instigation) president of the newly founded International Psychoanalytic Association. In eight years an informal group had become an international organization. As a measure of his growing international reputation, in 1909 Freud was invited to speak at Clark University in Worcester, Massachusetts, (his only American visit) and was awarded an honorary degree by that university.

With an international organization Freud now had more trouble on his hands than he wanted. His Viennese followers felt slighted by his promotion of Jung and others from Zurich. Freud made Adler president of the Vienna Society to balance things out. But he remained convinced that the association of psychoanalysis with Vienna was a handicap to the movement, and he wanted to turn the leadership over to a younger man who had energy and the talent to organize (42–43). In addition he wanted to remove psychoanalysis from its exclusively Jewish origins. It must not, he felt, be branded a Jewish science.

The secession of Adler and Jung occurred against the background of the strains between Vienna and Zurich. But Adler and Jung would have left the movement in any event. Both were intelligent and ambitious and, though genuinely involved in psychoanalysis for a time, wanted to develop their own ideas. This, said Freud, was fair enough, but ideas that discount some or all of the fundamental findings of psychoanalysis represent an "abandonment of analysis and a secession from it" (66). Freud is explicit about these fundamental findings: resistance and repression, the unconscious, infantile sexuality, and the interpretation of dreams (15–20). Adler, he thought, had abandoned repression and the unconscious for an ego psychology. Jung had redefined libido as a general nonerotic psychic force and had rejected infantile sexuality. Finally, the inevitable happened. Adler resigned from the Vienna Psychoanalytical Society in 1911. Jung resigned as president of the International Psychoanalytic Association in 1914. In each case the estrangement was both intellectual and personal. In particular Freud felt betrayed by Jung, in whom he had invested the future of psychoanalysis.[3] Even the case of the Wolf Man, as he admits in a footnote on the first page, is connected with *On the History of the Psycho-Analytic Movement* and "supplements the polemic contained in that essay" (*SE,* 17:7 n). In demonstrating the "significance of the infantile factor" in the Wolf Man's neurosis, Freud is addressing both Adler and Jung, but especially Jung (54).

It is easy to characterize these two secessions and the choosing of sides that accompanied them as the internal squabbles of a religious sect. It is also easy to characterize Freud as a dogmatist (as Jung did) who demanded rigid adherence to his ideas. I don't think either of these views is entirely correct, but it's possible to see how many people (especially critics of Freud) could hold one or both of them. Adler and Jung were going their own way no matter what. It seems to me impossible to read the Freud-Jung correspondence without concluding that Jung was looking for a fight and that, in fact, Freud conceded about as much as he could without abandoning his own basic views.

The problem lies in the consequences. Even before Jung had resigned, Ernest Jones had suggested the formation of a "tight, small organization of loyalists, a clandestine 'Committee,' to rally around Freud as his dependable palace guard." This Committee was to share news and ideas and to discuss privately any tendency to depart from the fundamental tenets of repression, the unconscious, or infantile sexuality (Gay 1988, 229–30). Freud accepted this idea, and the Committee of six was born.[4]

All of this is understandable in view of how beleaguered these early psychoanalysts felt. But it is not good science. In laying down certain basic views that could not be questioned, the Committee perpetuated a legacy of dogmatism that haunted many psychoanalysts for decades. For to question (or even seem to question) one or another of the core ideas determined the analyst's right to membership in the many psychoanalytic societies that accepted these ideas as fundamental. An analyst was either orthodox or not. Many, like Erich Fromm and Karen Horney, went their own way. Others kept their doubts to themselves (Erik H. Erikson, I think, is one of these) and remained within mainstream psychoanalysis. Thus, there was considerable restriction of freedom of inquiry for many analysts.

Unfortunately the Committee functioned for many years. It never succeeded fully, however, in protecting Freud from the exigencies of psychoanalytic organization. Even if only from a distance, he remained involved in organizational issues, in the founding and operation of a psychoanalytic press (1919), in attending international congresses, and (especially after World War I) in conducting the training analyses of aspiring psychoanalysts, many of these from America or England (like James and Alix Strachey, his future translators). In fact, these activities became as much a part of his life in psychoanalysis as did his clinical work and publications.

In the rest of this chapter I concentrate on four groups of Freud's publications: first, the papers on therapeutic technique; second, "On Narcissism: An Introduction"; third, one of the papers on metapsychology; and fourth, the two major books of this period, *Beyond the Pleasure Principle* and *Group Psychology and the Analysis of the Ego* (1921). I stress those works that are innovative and point to future change rather than those that summarize and consolidate previous views.

On Technique

Strachey lists 27 works by Freud dealing in whole or in part with therapeutic technique. Usually, however, reference to the technique papers means the series of six essays published from 1911 to 1915. These essays are evidently a substitute for a book entitled *General Methodology of Psycho-Analysis,* which Freud announces in "The Future Prospects of Psycho-Analytic Therapy" (1919) but never completes (*SE,* 11:142). The essays are thus Freud's closest approach to a systematic description of psychoanalytic technique.[5] They include discussions of many subjects—some of them very practical—that have guided psychoanalysts through most of this century.[6] I discuss only the three subjects that best illustrate Freud's change in technique since *Studies on Hysteria.*

First, Freud no longer begins the analysis with a focus on the symptoms and with the goal of clearing them up one by one. As early as the Dora case, he had already said that this technique is inadequate for "dealing with the finer structure of a neurosis." He now, he continues, lets "the patient himself choose the subject of the day's work, and in that way I start out from whatever surface his unconscious happens to be presenting to his notice at the moment" (*SE,* 7:12). In "On Beginning the Treatment" (1913), he continues to endorse this way of beginning both the treatment and each day's work: "What the material is with which one starts the treatment is on the whole a matter of indifference." The only exception is that the "fundamental rule of psychoanalytic technique" must be observed—that is, the patient must say everything that comes to mind no matter how trivial or unpleasant (*SE,* 12:134–35). The analyst's equivalent of the fundamental rule, he says in "Recommendations to Physicians Practicing Psycho-Analysis" (1912), is to listen with an "evenly-suspended attention" by which he will facilitate his unconscious memory of what the patient says (111–12).[7]

My second subject is transference. I have already mentioned Freud's first reference to transference in *Studies on Hysteria.* He refers to it again in a letter of 16 April 1900, in which he says of the long treatment of a patient called Herr E. that "I am beginning to understand that the apparent endlessness of the treatment is something that occurs regularly and is connected with the transference" (*Freud-Fliess,* 409). This is seven months before Dora enters analysis in October 1900 and, 11 weeks later, quits. In a postscript to Dora's case Freud ascribes this premature termination to his failure to master the transference "in good time" (*SE,* 7:118). Transferences, he says, are "new editions or facsimiles of the impulses and phantasies which are aroused and made conscious during the progress of the analysis" and which "replace some earlier person by the person of the physician" (116).

In retrospect Freud realizes that Dora had replaced at least two people by his person: her father and her father's friend Herr K. (with whose wife her father was having an affair). The transference was undoubtedly facilitated by several things. First, Dora had bad memories of previous doctors to whom she had been sent. Second, Dora believed (rightly) that her father wanted Freud to talk her out of her belief that Herr K. had made improper advances to her (the first when she was 14) and, further, that her father was willing to allow Herr K. such liberties as a kind of trade-off for his affair with Frau K. Thus Freud became a surrogate for the unbelieving or betraying father. And third, Dora plainly linked Freud with Herr K. as just another adult seducer. To his credit Freud recognized Dora's story about Herr K. as the truth, but he remained deaf (his word) to the transference and was surprised when she took revenge on him as she wanted to on Herr K. and walked out.[8]

In "The Dynamics of Transference" (1912), "Remembering, Repeating, and Working-Through" (1914), and "Observations on Transference-Love" (1915), Freud corrects his oversight in Dora's case. He now places the analysis of transference and resistance at the center of the therapeutic process. Why is transference connected to resistance? Because in therapy transference enters into relation with resistance. To explain the connection, Freud proposes three types of transference: a positive, conscious transference of friendly feelings for the analyst; a positive, unconscious transference of an erotic origin for the analyst; and a negative transference of hostile feelings for the analyst. The last two are suitable for resistance—the negative for obvious reasons, the positive because falling in love with the analyst ends the patient's interest in the treatment and is thus "an expression of resistance" (*SE,* 12:162).[9] They are usually encountered together as an ambivalent mixture of love and hate toward the analyst, though the positive transference usually appears first.

In Freud's therapy of this period, as he says, the original focus is no longer on remembering, either through hypnosis or free association. The focus, instead, is on making resistance conscious, thus freeing the patient to remember. It follows that making resistance conscious means making the transference conscious. In "Remembering, Repeating, and Working-Through," Freud says that the transference becomes conscious by creating in the analysis a transference neurosis—that is, by creating a new, artificial entity that replaces the patient's "ordinary" neurosis. This new illness (the third of my subjects) takes over all the features of the original illness, and from the "repetitive reactions which are exhibited in the transference we are led along the familiar paths to the awakening of the memories . . . after the resistance has been overcome" (154–55). In the transference neurosis (not to be confused with transference neuroses such as hysteria and obsession), as Ellman says, the patient supposedly brings to the treatment the "original conflicts that caused the symptoms." Thus, analysis uncovers the past in the present, since the patient relives his or her childhood in the transference neurosis—a matter of much debate among present-day analysts (Ellman, 23–33; quotation on 30).

But transference can also be dangerous, as Freud argues in "Observations on Transference-Love." The analyst must neither gratify nor suppress transference love. He must especially remember that the patient's love is an illusion and not attempt to base a real-life relationship on it. He must treat it as "something unreal" and assist the patient in bringing his or her unconscious erotic life into consciousness and so under control (*SE,* 12:166). Though he doesn't use the word here, Freud is implicitly warning analysts of their own countertransference—that is, their own unconscious emotional responses to the patient.[10]

In analyzing the transference—that new edition of old conflicts—symptoms are resolved by going back to their origin, renewing the conflict from which they began, and "with the help of motive forces which were not at the patient's disposal in the past, we must guide it to a different outcome." That different outcome is no less than a "revision of the process of repression," which is made possible by an alteration of the ego under the analyst's influence. By means of interpreting the transference neurosis the unconscious becomes conscious, and the "ego is enlarged at the cost of this unconscious." Symptom removal, then, is a kind of by-product of this change in the dynamic relation between conscious and unconscious, for the ego is now more "conciliatory" toward the libido, is "inclined to grant it some satisfaction," and "its repugnance to the claims of the libido is diminished by the possibility of disposing of a portion of it by sublimation." "When the libido is released once more from its temporary object in the person of the doctor," Freud says, "it cannot return to its earlier objects, but is at the disposal of the ego" (*SE,* 16:454–55).

Freud is generally no therapeutic optimist. As early as *Studies on Hysteria,* he speaks only of "transforming your hysterical misery into common unhappiness" (*SE,* 2:305). Nor, as he says in *New Introductory Lectures on Psycho-Analysis* (1933), is he a "therapeutic enthusiast" (*SE,* 22:151). As he makes clear in this work and the later "Analysis Terminable and Interminable" (1937), there are many limitations to the therapeutic power of psychoanalysis. Some neurotics cannot be cured, some therapists' efforts will fail, some will succeed—as in any medical situation. Yet he is convinced that psychoanalysis can cure some cases, that it can "get rid of disturbances and bring about changes for which in pre-analytic times one would not have ventured to hope" (153). Psychoanalysts generally accept the idea of the curative effect of psychoanalysis, many of them being much more optimistic than Freud about its effectiveness.

Yet the effectiveness of psychoanalysis as a therapy has been contested through the century and continues to be to the present. One of the basic assumptions of most recent criticism is the failure of psychoanalysis as a therapy. But even those who are not among the adversaries in the Freud wars are forced to very minimal, inconclusive positions. Paul Kline, for example, reports that, in an extensive survey of the literature on the efficacy of psychoanalytic therapy, he could find no study well enough designed to give unequivocal results. As he says, the "obstacles against obtaining adequate control groups, and the difficulties of measuring outcome, together with the need for good samples of patients and therapists have proved too great." Thus there is no proof of the effectiveness of psychoanalysis, but also no disproof (Kline 1984, 125).[11]

Freud generally believed that his and other analysts' sessions with patients were adequate proof of psychoanalytic ideas (Gay 1988, 523). In 1934 he wrote to Saul Rosenzweig about some experimental studies of Rosenzweig's verifying several psychoanalytic ideas. In this letter, Freud says that he sees little value in these studies "because the wealth of reliable observations" on which psychoanalysis is based "make them independent of experimental verification."[12] Most—but not all—psychoanalysts have followed Freud in taking the case study as adequate evidence of both therapeutic efficacy and confirmation of theory.

Today, many disagree with this position. Individuals, Bucci argues, may be convinced of the effectiveness of their own psychoanalytic treatment (as she is), but this conviction cannot be communicated to others who lack this experience. The need for evidence must be addressed, she concludes, or the field will remain confined to believers and be viewed by many as "somewhere between religion, cult, or fraud, or, at best, an interesting humanistic or literary enterprise and an important intellectual influence on 20th-century thought" (Bucci, 6). Both Eagle and Grünbaum argue that only extraclinical testing will do, because the clinical situation is contaminated by the patient's compliance and suggestibility and the therapist's theoretical biases (Eagle, 154–63; Grünbaum, passim). This is probably extreme, since some psychoanalytic concepts such as transference and resistance (in their psychoanalytic sense) may only be testable intraclinically. But the point about empirical verification remains as a serious challenge to psychoanalysis.[13]

It may be a serious challenge but, as Kline's survey of the literature shows, not an easy one to meet. Moreover, the problem may be more complex than simply developing well-designed studies. For example, Donald Spence argues that the research community is "doomed to junior partnership in the analytic enterprise" until it has "access to the private commentaries of the analyst." So long as "clinical research deals with incomplete data, its conclusions will never carry conviction, because the clinician can always say, with justification, that if all the facts were known, the conclusions would be different." Why are clinical data incomplete? Because, Spence says, no clinician remembers, notices, or interprets everything that occurs during an analytic session. All case histories are partial, anecdotal narratives that have been progressively smoothed out in the process of transcribing and publishing the case. And because clinical research "must necessarily study incomplete data, it can never take what may be its most important step—that of *disproving* a clinical hypothesis."[14] There is evidently a very wide gulf between Spence (with whom many, if not most, clinicians would probably agree) and the community of clinical researchers. There is also, as Spence admits, a gulf among clinicians, who often interpret the same case in very different ways and who, in addition, do not always agree on the criteria for cure.

Criteria for cure, indeed, are difficult to formulate. For Freud after 1900 (and for most psychoanalysts), the disappearance of symptoms is not an adequate criterion for cure. There must also be a fundamental change in the dynamic balance between the ego and the unconscious. This kind of characterological change requires insight by the patient into the resistance in the transference neurosis and a working through of this resistance according to the fundamental rule until the repressed instinctual impulses are discovered (*SE,* 12:154–56). The problem is that this insight is not the same for every patient. For Freud a normal ego is an "ideal fiction" (*SE,* 23:235). The difference between neurosis and health, he says, is a "practical question" and is defined by outcome—that is, "whether the subject is left with a sufficient amount of capacity for enjoyment and of efficiency" (*SE,* 16:457). Such an outcome, however, is bound to vary from subject to subject. This variability and the subjectivity of the kind of characterological change psychoanalysts seek in the analytic process strongly militate against the laying down of general, objective criteria of cure—or, at least, they have so far.

Bucci's plea for the necessity of testing the effectiveness of therapy is compelling, and she is surely correct that it is both urgent and essential for the health of psychoanalysis. In a time of psychotropic drugs and managed health care that wants effective and short-term treatment, it seems especially imperative that empirical evidence of the therapeutic efficacy of psychoanalysis be available. But it is hard to see how this evidence is to be reliably gathered.

On Narcissism

Freud published "On Narcissism: An Introduction" in 1914. But this essay does not represent his first interest in the subject. As Strachey says, Freud had told the Vienna Psychoanalytical Society on 10 November 1909 that a stage of narcissism was a necessary intermediate between autoerotism and object love (*SE,* 14:69). In the 1910 edition of *Three Essays on the Theory of Sexuality,* he adds a footnote on the "narcissistic basis" of homosexuality, in which a man identifies with a woman (usually his mother), takes himself as a sexual object, and then looks for a man who resembles him and whom he can love as his mother loved him (*SE,* 7:145). In the same year, in his essay on Leonardo, he describes Leonardo's finding of an object of love along a path of narcissism (*SE,* 11:100).[15] In the Schreber case of 1911, he describes a stage of narcissism between the stages of autoerotism and object love, indicates the possibility of a fixation at this stage, and suggests that male paranoids (like Schreber) regress to a fixation point "somewhere between the stages of auto-erotism, narcissism, and homosexuality" (*SE,* 12:62). Finally, in *Totem and Taboo* he refers to the overvaluation of their psychical acts by primitive men and neurotics as due to narcissism (*SE,* 13:88–90).

By the time of "On Narcissism," then, Freud has already discussed aspects of narcissism in a number of places. In this essay he now seeks theoretical clarification of the concept. And he begins with the psychosis that was then variously called dementia praecox or schizophrenia.[16] In view of Freud's limited experience with psychosis (Schreber was analyzed through his memoirs) and his conviction that psychotics could not be analyzed because they did not form transferences to the analyst, this is a curious starting point. He once even confessed to disliking psychotics (Gay 1988, 537). But he seems to have been challenged by Jung's assertion that libido theory could not explain the loss of reality in schizophrenia (*SE,* 14:79–80). Freud thinks otherwise. Schizophrenics, he says, "display two fundamental characteristics: megalomania and diversion of their interest from the external world—from people and things." Unlike hysterics and obsessives, who retain connections with objects in fantasy, the schizophrenic has really withdrawn from people and things "without replacing them by others in phantasy" (74). Observations of primitives and children, Freud says, reinforce what is seen in psychosis.

The question is, What happens to the withdrawn libido? The existence of megalomania gives Freud an answer. The withdrawn libido has been "directed to the ego and thus gives rise to an attitude which may be called narcissism." But this is only a secondary narcissism—a "magnification and plainer manifestation of a condition which had already existed previously." So the secondary condition is "superimposed upon a primary narcissism" (75). Thus, there is primary narcissism (a normal developmental stage) and secondary narcissism, which is regressive.

The addition of narcissism to the libido theory, however, is not the end of the matter. It raises a number of questions and problems, as well as new areas of interest. First, Freud wants to know the relationship of narcissism to autoerotism. His answer here is brief: the ego cannot be present from the beginning; it must develop. But autoerotism is present from the beginning. Hence, to bring about narcissism, a new psychical action (presumably a rudimentary ego) must be added (77). Yet in *Introductory Lectures on Psycho-Analysis,* he says that autoerotism is the "sexual activity of the narcissistic stage of allocation of the libido" (*SE,* 16:416).

This second statement is clearly more compatible with a stage of primary narcissism prior to object relations.[17]

The second question is a pivotal one in the history of psychoanalysis, for it will lead to the revision of instinct theory in *Beyond the Pleasure Principle:* if there is such a thing as primary ego libido, "why is there any necessity for further distinguishing a sexual libido from a non-sexual energy of the ego-instincts?" (*SE,* 14:76). As I have already indicated, Freud had identified two instincts prior to 1914: the sexual instinct or libido (love) and the ego or self-preservative instinct (hunger). But this duality is now threatened by the theory of narcissism. For, as Wollheim says, "if there is an original libidinal attachment to the ego, is it not plausible to think that the self-preservative instincts express or derive from this attachment, and do not represent an independent or nonsexual form of drive?" (Wollheim, 204). Not only would the "postulation of a single kind of psychical energy" leave Freud with a definition of libido identical to Jung's (*SE,* 14:76), it would also jeopardize his conception of the repressed and repressing forces in the creation of neurosis.

This dilemma remains unresolved until Freud's new dualism of life and death instincts in 1920. Until then he can only try to maintain both the idea of the ego instincts and of ego libido. So, in *Introductory Lectures on Psycho-Analysis,* he tries an interesting gambit. Energy sent out from the ego toward the object of its sexual desire, he says, is libido. Any other energies sent out from the ego (which he terms "interest") "are sent out by the self-preservative instincts" (*SE,* 16:414). But interest remains undefined and unspecified. This is at best a rearguard action. For, with the recognition that the energy of the ego is really libidinal in origin, Freud's opposition of ego and libido instincts is finally untenable and, like it or not, his position is indistinguishable from Jung's.

My third subject is not a problem but a new direction. In studying narcissism Freud encounters a subject that will increasingly move to the center of his interest—the subject of how the ego makes object choices. This subject, of course, pervades the essay, since narcissism is after all a retreat from object choice. But it comes up in a very specific way in Freud's discussion of the "erotic life of human beings, with its many kinds of differentiation in man and woman." Freud discusses two types of object choice in love. The first is the anaclitic or attachment type, in which persons (usually the mother) concerned with a "child's feeding, care, and protection become his earliest sexual objects" (*SE,* 14:87). The second type is the narcissistic, in which the person takes as an object, not his mother, but his own self. As Freud says, the fact of narcissistic object choice is the "strongest of the reasons which have led us to adopt the hypothesis of narcissism" (88). Both types, he says, are open to both men and women, though women tend to favor a narcissistic object choice.

Of the varieties of narcissistic object choices, Freud singles out one—the narcissist who loves himself as he would like to be—for special attention. Which leads to my fourth subject—the introduction of the ego ideal, the forerunner of the superego. The ego ideal, he says, is the "target of the self-love which was enjoyed in childhood by the actual ego." As the child grows up and is "disturbed by the admonitions of others and by the awakening of his own critical judgment"—that is, as he leaves the stage of primary narcissism—he can no longer retain the "narcissistic perfection of his childhood" and so seeks to recover it in the form of the ego ideal. What the person "projects before him as his ideal is the substitute for the lost narcissism of his childhood in which he was his own ideal" (94). There may even be a "special psychical agency" that seeks to assure the narcissistic satisfaction of the ego ideal and that "constantly watches the actual ego and measures it by that ideal" (95). This must, Freud says, be our conscience, which arises from the critical influence of the child's parents and others who teach and train the child, from other people in general, and from "public opinion" (96).

In "On Narcissism," then, Freud theoretically clarifies a new concept, adds a new stage of libidinal development, begins the process of revising instinct theory, begins to pay increased attention to the ego and its object relations, and introduces one of the components of what will become the structural theory in 1923. It is, indeed, a watershed essay.

On Metapsychology

In the spring and summer of 1915 Freud began to write a systematic statement of the theory of psychoanalysis. He planned a series of 12 interrelated papers that were to be published as a book. Of these 12 essays three were published as separate pieces in 1915, and two in 1917. The other seven were never published. Six were lost or destroyed and one—the draft called "A Phylogenetic Fantasy"—was, as I have mentioned, found among Ferenczi's letters and published. Presumably Freud was not satisfied with his treatment of consciousness, conversion hysteria, obsession, and the transference neuroses in general—the subjects of the lost essays. The five published essays are "Instincts and Their Vicissitudes," "Repression," "The Unconscious," "A Metapsychological Supplement to the Theory of Dreams," and "Mourning and Melancholia." These five works are usually referred to as the metapsychological essays, and each is a major document in the history of psychoanalysis.[18] I have already referred to the first three in discussing theoretical issues in the last chapter. In this section I focus on "Mourning and Melancholia" as the essay that continues the transition in Freud's thought begun in "On Narcissism."

This transitional trend appears in "Mourning and Melancholia" as a deepening interest in object relations and a further elaboration of the ego ideal. Both mourning and melancholia (today called depression) show the same features: painful dejection, a loss of interest in the world, a loss of the ability to love, a cessation of activity. But melancholics also display "a lowering of the self-regarding feelings to a degree that finds utterance in self-reproaches and self-revilings, and culminates in a delusional expectation of punishment" (*SE,* 14:244). In mourning there is no disturbance of self-regard. In time, when the work of mourning is over, the "ego becomes free and uninhibited again" (245). But melancholia persists, as do its remorseless self-reproaches. And yet there is "no correspondence . . . between the degree of self-abasement and its real justification" (247). Indeed, the melancholic's self-reproaches hardly fit him or her at all. But they do fit someone else—"someone whom the patient loves or has loved or should love." The self-reproaches are "reproaches against a loved object which have been shifted away from it on to the patient's own ego" (248). Thus, Freud says in one of his most famous sentences, the "shadow of the object fell upon the ego, and the latter could henceforth be judged by a special agency, as though it were an object, the forsaken object" (249). Though not named, the special agency is the ego ideal, which Freud refers to as conscience in this essay and which will next appear in *Group Psychology and the Analysis of the Ego.*

But this falling of the shadow of the object on the ego leads to two questions. First, how does it occur? The answer is that libido freed from the object is withdrawn into the ego (that is, there is a narcissistic regression) and serves "to establish an *identification* of the ego with the abandoned object." Identification—a term that grows in importance—Freud defines as a "preliminary stage of object choice," the first way the ego chooses an object. The ego wants to "incorporate this object into itself" and so, in its earliest effort to do so in the oral stage, "it wants to do so by devouring it" (249–50; Freud's italics). This primitive oral incorporation is the prototype of all later identifications, which always involve some form of internalizing or introjecting of objects.

The second question is, Why does the melancholic direct reproaches toward this object? Here, the answer is that the loss of a love object is "an excellent opportunity for the ambivalence in love-relationships to make itself effective and come into the open" (250–51). In melancholia, Freud says, there is a double regression: to narcissistic identification, where hatred of the object appears; and to the stage of anal sadism. The hatred comes, not from the sadism directed against the object, but, as Freud argues in "Instincts and Their Vicissitudes," from the ego. An instinct cannot love or hate, he says. Only a total ego can. So love and hate come from the ego, not, like sadism, from an instinct. And, Freud further argues, the ego's relation to the stimuli of the external world—including people—is one of hatred before it is one of love. "Hate," he says, "as a relation to objects, is older than love. It derives from the narcissistic ego's primordial repudiation of the external world with its outpouring of stimuli" (139).[19] Thus, in melancholia, both sadism and hate are directed at the internalized object, which, though loved, has also "slighted, neglected or disappointed" the person in numerous ways (251).

Eros and Thanatos

If Freud had a radically speculative bent that he tried to curb by restricting himself to careful observation, he clearly shows it in *Beyond the Pleasure Principle.* What follows, he says at one point, "is speculation, often far-fetched speculation" (*SE,* 18:24). And speculation it is, imagining as he does a kind of epic account of how lumps of organic matter, assailed by noxious stimuli from the environment, repeatedly returned to their nonorganic origins, then became organic again, then nonorganic, and so on over unknown numbers of years. The result: all protoplasm has an inborn tendency to return to the state from which it arose—to die. This is the death instinct, which pervades all of organic life.[20] Although Freud says near the end of the book that he is "not convinced" of his argument for the death instinct and does not seek to persuade others, he does use the idea regularly in many of his later works as if it were fully established in his own mind (59).

It is surprising to learn that the idea of a death instinct was neither original with Freud nor new to psychoanalysis. As early as 1911, Sabina Spielrein (1885–1941) read to the Vienna Psychoanalytical Society a portion of a paper later published as "Destruction as the Cause of Coming into Being" (1912). In this paper she spoke of a death instinct as proposed by Russian biologist and founder of immunology (Spielrein was Russian) Ilya Mechnikov (1845–1916). The published article, say Appignanesi and Forrester, "had the unenviable and perhaps unique fate of being a major influence on both Freud and Jung" (Appignanesi and Forrester, 216).[21]

It is not surprising, however, to discover that Freud bases his idea of the death instinct on one of his fundamental ideas—the constancy principle, which he here attributes to Gustav Theodor Fechner (1801–1887), the founder of psychophysics. From the idea that the "mental apparatus endeavors to keep the quantity of excitation present in it as low as possible or at least to keep it constant" (the Nirvana principle, he now calls it), it is not too great a leap to argue that "*an instinct is an urge inherent in organic life to restore an earlier state of things*" (*SE,* 18:9, 36; Freud's italics). Instincts, then, are conservative. They strive after old things.[22] The final goal of all organic striving—the ultimate tension reduction—is to die. Hence the " '*aim of all life is death*' " (38; Freud's italics).

Given that one of the props of this argument is an invalid biological assumption—the constancy principle or principle of tension reduction—Freud's idea of the death instinct runs into immediate problems, which were already implicit in the principle of neuronal inertia in the *Project.* There is, say Slavin and Kriegman, a principle of nature that parallels Freud's death instinct—the Second Law of Thermodynamics, which governs all matter as it moves toward entropy. But the Second Law, they argue, is neither a biological principle nor an instinct. In fact, biological entities (though they ultimately conform to the Second Law) are capable of opposing entropy and passing on genes to create new entities. There is, they conclude, "no reason whatsoever for organisms to be motivated to promote the Second Law of Thermodynamics" (Slavin and Kriegman, 216).

But Freud's argument is not entirely dependent on the principle of constancy. Part of it is based on empirical observation. In such phenomena as posttraumatic dreams in which the traumatic situation is repeated (in, for example, the war neuroses of World War I), in children's play, in the need of neurotic patients to repeat the past, and in people seemingly doomed to repeat past mistakes, Freud sees a repetition compulsion that he regards as a demonic (his word) power compelling people to seek unpleasure rather than pleasure.[23] So these phenomena go beyond the pleasure principle. The ultimate repetition is, of course, to restore an earlier state of things. The repetition compulsion—based supposedly on observed phenomena and so not speculative—

together with the constancy principle constitutes proof of the death instinct.

Many psychoanalysts have had trouble with Freud's view of the repetition compulsion as "something that seems more primitive, more elementary, more instinctual than the pleasure principle which it overrides" (*SE,* 18:23). For one thing, neurotic repetition is expected in a person who is caught in a conflict between the ego and a sexual instinct. But such a conflict doesn't go beyond the pleasure principle. It is intrinsically a conflict between the pleasure and the reality principles and is acted out repetitively in the transference neurosis. Max Schur argues that Freud simply uses various aspects of unpleasurable repetition to confirm a hypothesis he has already formulated. Even Freud's main evidence for the repetition compulsion—traumatic dreams—can be interpreted as the ego's unconscious wish to undo the trauma by reliving it over and over rather than the ego's dominance by this compulsion.[24]

But the constancy principle and the repetition compulsion do not complete Freud's evidence. To get to his final evidence it is necessary first to ask the question, If there is a death instinct why do organisms live at all? Why don't they just die? Freud's answer is that there is a force that opposes the death instinct and that it must have been present from the beginning of life. That force is libido, which partly neutralizes the death instinct by binding individual cells into multicellular organisms as a "means of prolonging their life." In this way, he concludes, the "libido of our sexual instincts would coincide with the Eros of the poets and philosophers which holds all living things together" (50).

Believing that biology says little about the origins of sexuality, Freud takes a hint from Plato about its beginning. In Plato's *Symposium* Aristophanes advances the theory that primitive humans were originally man, woman, and the union of the two and that each person was divided by Zeus into halves each of which sought reunion with its lost part. Could it be, Freud asks, that "living substance" was torn apart as it came to life and has since "endeavored to reunite through the sexual instincts"? (58). But here he breaks off. Nevertheless, he continues to define love in a very wide sense—self-love, love of parents and children, friendship, love of humanity, and devotion to concrete objects and abstract ideas (90). Thus, what psychoanalysis calls sexuality is "by no means identical with the impulsion towards a union of the two sexes." It is much more like the "all-inclusive and all-preserving Eros of Plato's *Symposium*" (*SE,* 19:218). Eros operates from the beginning of life as the life instinct that opposes the death instinct. Freud is now comfortably back with his old dualistic view (and saved from Jung's monistic libido theory), but now the conflict is between life and death instincts rather than ego and sexual instincts (*SE,* 18:53).[25]

Having established this new dualism, Freud is able to offer what he takes to be further empirical evidence for the existence of the death instinct. His evidence is sadism, hitherto described as a perversion and a component instinct of the pregenital anal stage. Is it not more plausible, he asks, to suppose that sadism is actually a death instinct that "has been forced away from the ego and has consequently only emerged in relation to the object?" (54). If so, then masochism is the primary instinct directed against the organism, and sadism would represent the death instinct turned outward (a reversal of the position taken in *Three Essays.*) Though the reasoning is circular—he can define sadism as aggression turned outward only by having first assumed the death instinct—Freud continues in future works to use sadism as the primary clinical evidence for the existence of the death instinct.[26]

I think it is fair to say that psychoanalysts have nearly universally rejected the idea of the death instinct, though it has been taken seriously by such cultural critics as Herbert Marcuse and Norman O. Brown.[27] Freud's new instinct theory did accomplish one thing: it placed the issue of aggression, along with sexuality, at the center of psychoanalytic thought. Even so, however, there is no unanimity among analysts as to the instinctual nature of aggression.[28]

On Group Psychology

Strachey observes that there is little direct connection between *Group Psychology and the Analysis of the Ego* and *Beyond the Pleasure Principle* (*SE,* 18:67–68). That isn't entirely true. The sexual instinct broadened into Eros is central to *Group Psychology.* And the death instinct makes a brief, disguised appearance. But it is true that Freud is now more concerned in following up his earlier interest in the ego, in identification, and in the ego ideal than he is with instinct theory. Together, both works clearly point forward to *The Ego and the Id.*

Freud begins by collapsing the contrast between the individual and the social in group psychology. In the individual's mental life, he argues, someone else is always involved—"as a model, as an object, as a helper, as an opponent"—so that what is individual is also social (69). The social instinct, then, may be further reducible rather than primary; indeed, Freud's expectation is "that it may be possible to discover the beginnings of its development in a narrower circle, such as that of the family" (70).[29]

Freud next turns to a consideration of two works of social psychology: Gustave Le Bon's *The Crowd: A Study of the Popular Mind* (1895) and William McDougal's *The Group Mind* (1920). Both writers, he notes, focus on the primitive and childish behavior of groups (crowd or mob would be a better word). Both believe that in a group the individual is lacking in critical ability, is highly suggestible, and is often violent and irrational. Yet both writers also recognize that the morals of a group may be higher than those of the individuals who compose it. McDougal sees the difference as lying in stability or organization. But, as Freud implies when he turns to his two representative artificial groups—the Catholic Church and the army—organization and stability are not necessarily different in the dynamics of their influence over individuals from those of the more transient, less organized mob. Freud wants to know what holds all groups together. Freud also observes that neither Le Bon nor McDougal gives attention to the difference between leaderless groups and those with leaders. He will, he says, concentrate on groups with leaders, as his two "communities of believers," the church and the army, show (93).[30] What these two groups share is the "illusion" of there being a leader "who loves all the individuals in the group with an equal love" (94). In addition, each individual in these groups is bound to the "other members of the group" (95).

Freud offers two theories to account for groups with leaders and strong emotional ties by individuals to each other and to the leader. One, as Wallace says, is biogenetic (Wallace, 248–49). The human group, Freud says, "appears to us as a revival of the primal horde." By revival Freud means a phylogenetically inherited survival of a prehistoric essential experience. Primitive man, he says, survives in each person, and the "primal horde may arise once more out of any random collection" (*SE,* 18:123). The sons, of course, feared the primal father. So the loving leader of church and army is "simply an idealistic remodelling of the state of affairs in the primal horde, where all of the sons knew that they were equally *persecuted* by the primal father, and *feared* him equally" (124–25; Freud's italics). Indeed, the idealistic remodeling is already apparent in the totemic clans where the slain father is worshipped as the totem animal.

Freud's second theory of the group is psychological. He begins by using the concept of libido/Eros to study group psychology—with the supposition that "love relationships" are the "essence of the group mind" (91). When a group is formed, he argues, all hostility among group members vanishes (at least temporarily)—a limitation of self-love that can only suggest a love of others (102). And he describes two mechanisms for the creation of this love of others in the group: identification and being in love.

In "Mourning and Melancholia" identification is a mechanism that establishes an internalization of an object that is then persecuted by the ego ideal. But in *Group Psychology* Freud greatly expands the idea of identification in his longest discussion of it anywhere in his work. Here the introjection of the object into the ego as a "substitute for a libidinal object-tie" (as in melancholia) is only one of three sources of identification (108). Another is the identification of the boy (Freud is not yet ready to consider the girl) with the father. This identification, he says, occurs simultaneously with, or a bit earlier than, the boy's "true object-cathexis" toward his mother. The Oedipus complex originates from the "confluence" of the two ties. Noticing that his father stands between him and his mother, the boy's father identification becomes hostile. Identification, then, "is ambivalent from the very first" (105). What is new in this discussion is that Freud now sees identification as an element in the Oedipus complex—a discovery that he will clarify in *The Ego and the Id.* Finally, there is identification with "some other person who is not an object of the sexual instinct." The "mutual tie between members of a group," Freud says, is of the third kind (108). But the first of these types of identification, where the ego has been "altered by introjection and . . . contains the lost object" so that one part (the ego ideal) "rages" against the other, also plays a role in the formation of a group (109).

In addition to identification, being in love is another obvious way of forming emotional ties. Here the Oedipus complex makes another appearance. By the time a child is five years old, he has found his first love in one of his parents (I clarify this odd statement in the next chapter). With repression of this infantile sexual aim the child remains tied to the parents by instincts that are aim-inhibited—that is, no longer sexual but affectionate (111). Affection is thus transformed sexuality—the first point in Freud's analysis. The second point is that in love we tend to overvalue the loved object. We idealize him or her. In many cases the loved object serves as a "substitute for some unattained ego ideal of our own." In some cases the loved object becomes more and more precious "until at last it gets possession of the entire self-love of the ego. . . . The object has, so to speak, consumed the ego" (112–13). This replacement happens also, Freud says, in hypnotism—a "group formation with two members" and different from a group only in number of people and from love only in lacking a sexual aim (115).

Freud is now ready to describe the dynamics of a primary group—that is, the emotional tie to the leader and to the other members of the group. The relation to the leader is the equivalent of the idealization of being in love. The relation to the members of the group is the result of an aim-inhibited (affectionate) identification. A primary group, then, "*is a number of individuals who have put one and the same object in the place of their ego ideal and have consequently identified with one another in their ego*" (116; Freud's italics). Social ties, then, are libidinal. In Freud's view no purely rational, self-interested social contract is sufficient to explain the compelling emotional bonds that hold people together. Nor does anything like a primary social instinct have any meaning for him.

Unfortunately, however, this emergence of such libidinal ties in what Freud calls a common group is regressive. The individual is too weak to do anything by himself or herself and must be reinforced in his or her emotional and intellectual activities by other members of the group. Pulled by the group toward its own prejudices and opinions and hypnotically dependent on the leader, who now represents the ego ideal, it is not surprising that individuals in a group are weak intellectually, emotionally unrestrained, incapable of moderation and delay, and inclined "to exceed every limit in the expression of emotion and to work it off completely in the form of action" (117).[31] Only in organized groups like the army and the church can these regressive tendencies be to a large extent checked. Yet even these organized groups exhibit the dynamics of the common, transient, or less organized groups. Human beings, as Freud would have it, are horde animals.

But where is the newly discovered death instinct or its derivative, external aggression? I think it is here, but only implicitly—as if Freud hasn't yet thought through its implications for understanding the group. Trying to determine when something like Trotter's herd instinct appears, Freud decides that it first appears in a nursery containing many children. The eldest child is envious of his younger siblings. But because his parents love the younger children as well as him, he cannot maintain his hostility without doing damage to himself, so he is "forced into identifying with the other children." Thus, a "communal or group feeling" develops that is increased in school. "What appears later on in society in the shape of *Gemeingeist, esprit de corps,* 'group spirit,' etc., does not belie its derivation from what was originally envy" (120). Social feeling, then, represents the reversal of a "hostile feeling into a positively-toned tie in the nature of an identification" (121). I see this brief analysis of the hostile basis of the social tie as a first, tentative step toward the analysis of aggression and guilt in *Civilization and Its Discontents.*

Chapter Five

The Final Period (1923–1939)

Two events stand out in 1923, both in April. On 20 April, Freud had the first operation on his jaw and palate for a leukoplastic lesion that proved to be malignant. In late April *The Ego and the Id* was published. Two other operations followed in October, both of them drastic attempts to resect the cancerous growth. A fourth operation followed in November. From 1923 on Freud continued to develop benign leukoplakias (undoubtedly a result of his continued addiction to cigars), which were removed in more than 30 operations (some of them more than minor). In order to keep the oral and nasal cavities separate, he was forced to wear a rubber prosthesis, which was painful to put in and take out (a job that fell to his daughter, Anna) and highly irritating to wear. He was in pain almost continuously but refused medication. In 1936 another operation revealed a recurrence of the cancer. It was a recurrence of this same cancer in 1939—this time inoperable—that led Freud to hold his physician, Max Schur, to his promise to end Freud's life when the pain became senseless and unbearable. On 21 September, Schur injected Freud with an overdose of morphine, repeated the injection when Freud became restless, and administered a final injection on 22 September. Freud died on 23 September in the London to which he had come as a refugee from Nazi Vienna.[1]

How Freud managed to see patients (now five days a week instead of six) and write is hard to imagine. But he did, and much of what he wrote is among his most interesting and controversial work. In this chapter I focus on the last of his major theoretical works—*The Ego and the Id* and *Inhibitions, Symptoms, and Anxiety.* I also discuss his final formulation of the Oedipus complex, including his ideas on the feminine. I then briefly discuss the last of Freud's writings on technique and his last three on culture—*The Future of an Illusion* (1927), *Civilization and Its Discontents,* and *Moses and Monotheism.*

The Structural Theory

The Ego and the Id is a watershed work in the history of psychoanalysis—for many analysts, indeed, a paradigm shift. It isn't really a paradigm shift, simply the culmination of Freud's increasing interest in the ego over the preceding nine years. But this statement in no way minimizes the importance of the book in Freud's thought or the history of psychoanalysis.[2]

In addition to containing Freud's ideas on the development of the ego, identification, and the ego ideal, *The Ego and the Id* also represents Freud's attempt to address two difficulties with his topographical and dynamic views of the unconscious. The first difficulty is unconscious fantasies, which are unconscious dynamically (that is, repressed) but which are, as Freud says in "The Unconscious," "highly organized, free from self-contradiction, have made use of every acquisition of the system *Cs.* and would hardly be distinguished in our judgment from the formations of that system." Qualitatively, then, they belong to the system Pcs. but factually to the Ucs. (*SE,* 14:190–91).[3] These fantasies, as Fancher says, are organized and noncontradictory, involve little condensation or displacement, and take account of both time and reality—in short, they lack the characteristics of the primary process. Fancher suggests the fantasies underlying the Oedipus complex as examples, for they involve a "realistic appraisal of the same-sexed parent as a more powerful rival." A representative of the Ucs., he says, "should theoretically not manifest such a concern for possible realistic consequences or such a high degree of logical structure" (Fancher 1973, 199–200). The antagonism between preconscious and unconscious may not be as absolute as Freud has hitherto thought.

The second difficulty arises from a closer scrutiny of the nature of resistance. It is, after all, not only the contents of the unconscious that are repressed; it is also true that the resistance emanating from the ego is unconscious. As he says, we "have come upon something in the ego itself which is also unconscious, which behaves exactly like the repressed." Instead of a split between conscious and unconscious, there is a different antithesis—that "between the coherent ego and the repressed which is split off from it" (*SE,* 19:17). So a part of the ego belongs to the unconscious, not the preconscious, and this fact is a fundamental challenge to the topography of conscious, preconscious, and unconscious. The structural view of the mind presented in *The Ego and the Id* is Freud's response to this challenge and his final model of the psychic apparatus.

Of the three components of the structural theory, two (the ego and the id) are adapted from earlier theory, and the third (the superego) is new. Since a part of the ego is unconscious, Freud can no longer speak of the system Ucs. He needs a new term to denote the systematic unconscious, and this term—*das Es* (the it, but translated by Strachey as id)—he borrows from Georg Groddeck's (1866–1934) *The Book of the It* (1923). The id, Freud says in his fullest discussion in *New Introductory Lectures on Psycho-Analysis,* is a "dark, inaccessible part of our personality." It is a "chaos, a cauldron full of seething excitations." It is filled with energy (unbound) from the instincts, obeys no logical laws (including that of contradiction), knows no negation, ignores space and time, and knows no judgments of value, good or evil, or morality. "Instinctual cathexes seeking discharge—that, in our view, is all there is in the id," Freud concludes.[4] We know the id only through the processes of the dream work and neurotic symptoms (*SE,* 22:73–74). Except for the addition of the death instinct as one of the two instincts, there is nothing in *The Ego and the Id* that differs from Freud's conception of the systematic unconscious in "The Unconscious" eight years earlier.

The second component of the structural theory is the ego (*das Ich,* the I, but translated by Strachey as ego). But though the ego is the psychic structure that functions according to the reality principle and operates logically and verbally, it is no longer an ego instinct. It is not even present at birth, when there is only id.[5] Hence it is a portion of the id that has been "modified by the direct influence of the external world" (*SE,* 19:25). Thus, it begins as the perception of stimuli from the external world, and from this function consciousness develops.[6] It is also a body ego, the surface of the body being a place "from which both external and internal perceptions may spring" (25). As this last statement suggests, the ego also receives internal stimuli—that is, excitations arising from the id. And by exercising thought it controls the motility of the organism toward the outside world. In short, it substitutes the reality for the pleasure principle—but always with an eye to eventual instinctual satisfaction. Finally, that portion of the ego that is unconscious functions as a defense against instinctual impulses and, though Freud doesn't say so, presumably gives structure to unconscious fantasies.[7] The full ego, then, includes perception, consciousness, the preconscious of the topographic view, and the dynamically unconscious function of repression. It "represents what may be called reason and common sense, in contrast to the id, which contains the passions" (25).

The third component of the structural theory is the superego, first named as such in *The Ego and the Id* and replacing the ego ideal as Freud's preferred term (though in this book he uses both). It is now advanced as a psychic agency equal in importance to the ego and the id. In *New Introductory Lectures on Psycho-Analysis* Freud defends his view that conscience is not simply a special agency in the ego. It is "more prudent," he says, to keep the superego as a separate agency that observes and judges the ego. A person may be inclined toward something that will give pleasure, but conscience (something separate from the ego) does not allow it. Or the same person may do something pleasurable for which conscience causes a feeling of remorse. What the ego perceives as unconflicted pleasure, conscience sees as forbidden. In addition there are the "delusions of being observed" experienced by paranoids, where being observed is a preparation for "judging and punishing." There is the persecution of the ego in melancholia (*SE,* 22:59–61). And there is the negative therapeutic reaction in patients who, from an unconscious sense of guilt, refuse to give up the "punishment of suffering" (*SE,* 19:49-50). Each of these phenomena shows the superego as independent of the ego. Freud thus concludes that, though this agency begins as a grade or differentiation in the ego, it should be understood as an agency separate from the ego.

In *Group Psychology* Freud first connects identification and the Oedipus complex. In *The Ego and the Id* he completes this connection by deriving the superego from the dissolution of the Oedipus complex. As does Freud, I will take the case of the boy as an example. At an early age, he says, the boy develops an object cathexis to the mother's breast—the "prototype of an object-choice on the anaclitic model." He identifies with his father, whom he internalizes as an idealized image of himself—as we know from "On Narcissism," the prototype of narcissistic object choice. The Oedipus complex originates when the boy perceives his father as an obstacle to his sexual wishes for the mother. His identification with his father becomes hostile and becomes a wish to "get rid of his father in order to take his place with his mother." The boy is now ambivalent toward his father. The "simple positive Oedipus complex" in a boy, then, includes ambivalence toward the father and the "object-relation of a solely affectionate kind" to his mother. At this point either the identification with the father intensifies or there is an identification with the mother. Freud regards the former "as the more normal" outcome because it allows the continuation of the affectionate feelings for the mother (31–32). The result is the dissolution of the Oedipus complex by the identification with the father forming a precipitate in the ego—the ego ideal or superego, which now confronts the ego.

This superego, says Freud, is not simply a "residue" of early object choice. It is also a reaction formation against these choices. It does not simply say to the ego that " 'You *ought to be* like this (like your father)' "; it says " 'You *may not be* like this (like your father).' " Just as the parents are viewed as an obstacle to the child's Oedipal wishes, "so his infantile ego fortified itself for the carrying out of the repression by erecting this same obstacle within itself" (34; Freud's italics). The ego ideal is thus the "heir of the Oedipus complex" (36). It borrows the strength to repress the Oedipus complex from the father, whose authority is continued under the influence of other authorities—religion, school, and reading (34–35).[8] The superego is thus the agency through which cultural norms and values are transmitted. It is a result of two related factors: a biologically long period of dependence and the Oedipus complex (35).

But why does the identification with the father lead to a new psychical agency of such power? For a part of the answer to this question I must look forward to Freud's "The Dissolution of the Oedipus Complex," in which he considers the reason for the repression of the Oedipus complex. In this essay he argues that what brings about the "destruction of the child's phallic genital organization" is the "threat of castration" (*SE,* 19:175).[9] This threat occurs in two ways: first, the parents threaten castration if the boy doesn't cease genital manipulation; and second, the sight of the female genitals reinforces this threat (174–76). If, as Freud says, the satisfaction of his Oedipal love is to cost him his penis, a conflict arises "between his narcissistic interest in that part of his body and the libidinal cathexis of his parental objects." In this conflict the "child's ego turns away from the Oedipus complex." The authority of the father (or the parents) is "introjected into the ego" and forms the nucleus of the superego that perpetuates the father's "prohibition against incest." The result is a repression of the Oedipus complex—indeed, of childhood sexuality as a whole—and a period of sexual latency that lasts until puberty. Ideally, he argues, more than repression occurs—there is actually a destruction or abolition of the complex. For if the ego does not achieve more than repression of the complex, "the latter persists in an unconscious state in the id and will later manifest its pathogenic effect" (176–77). The difference between repression and dissolution is the borderline between normality and pathology.[10] Freud's belief in the influence of the past—especially the first five years of life—in both normal and abnormal development is nowhere clearer than in this formulation.

Before turning to a consideration of the ego's relationship to the id, the superego, and external reality, I must make two further points about the superego and then pose a question about Freud's variable and often contradictory statements about identification. The first point is that, though in melancholia and obsession, guilt and remorse are conscious, for Freud a "great part of the sense of guilt must normally remain unconscious." The Oedipus complex, with which the origin of consciousness is connected, belongs to the unconscious. In hysteria guilt is unconscious. And in many criminals, an unconscious sense of guilt exists before the crime (51–52). Second, there is no superego prior to the repression of the Oedipus complex—a view later challenged by Melanie Klein.[11] As for identification, in chapter 3 of *The Ego and the Id* Freud says that in the beginning (the oral stage) "object-cathexis and identification are no doubt indistinguishable from each other" (29). This identification is not the outcome of an object cathexis; it is the "first and most important identification" of the child with his father, a "direct and immediate identification and takes place earlier than any object-cathexis" (31). Yet at the beginning of chapter 5 he reverts to the position of "Mourning and Melancholia" that the ego is formed out of identifications that replace abandoned object cathexes and that the "first of these identifications always behave as a special agency in the ego and stand apart from the ego in the form of a super-ego" (48). Mitchell argues that in the first statement Freud is considering "some sort of primary object relatedness as a basic motivational factor" but that he chooses not to follow that option. Thus, the third statement, in which identification is a result of the abandoned libidinal object of the Oedipus complex, allows Freud to maintain his commitment to drive theory (Mitchell 1988, 48–51; quotation on 49). Mitchell may or may not be right about Freud's consideration of primary object relatedness. The passages in question are very unclear. If the identification leading to the formation of the superego and so dissolving the Oedipus complex is the first, what has happened to the pre-Oedipal identification resulting in the ego ideal as described in *Group Psychology?* Freud is silent on this contradiction. But clearly he remains committed to his view that object relations are secondary to drive satisfaction.

The Ego and Its Relationships

At one point in *The Ego and the Id* Freud pictures the relation of the ego to the id as that of a man on horseback trying to hold back the superior strength of the horse. But the rider has his own strength, while the ego "uses borrowed forces." The ego, like the rider who often has to guide his horse where the horse wants to go, must transform the "id's will into action as if it was its own" (25). But as the source of the instincts and hence the source of all motivation, the id is always in a powerful position against the ego, which can only control or carry out the aims of the instincts.

In addition to the id, the superego also stands apart from and masters the ego. Just as the child "was once under a compulsion to obey its parents, so the ego submits to the categorical imperative of its super-ego" (48). As a result of the instinctual defusion that occurs in identification, the sadistic component of the sexual instinct (hitherto directed externally bound with Eros) entrenches itself in the superego and turns against the ego. The superego becomes a "pure culture of the death instinct" and is thus always close to the id (53).[12]

In Freud's view, though the ego has important functions in perception, mobility, defense against external and internal stimuli, and reality testing, it is in fact a "poor creature owing service to three masters and consequently menaced by three dangers: from the external world, from the libido of the id, and from the severity of the super-ego" (56). Having divested it of its own energy by redefining it as psychic agency rather than ego instinct, Freud is sensitive to the claim that the ego lacks any source of energy in its new form.[13] Nevertheless, it is this "poor creature" that has the task of bringing harmony to the internal and external forces acting on it. Psychoanalysis, he says, "is an instrument to enable the ego to achieve a progressive conquest of the id" (56). Or, in the more famous formula, "Where id was, there ego shall be" (*SE,* 22:80).[14] But the superego may also make powerful and relentless demands on the ego. It may even "make common cause" with the id against the ego. The analyst may, then, also have to come to the aid of the ego against both of its enemies in this civil war—the "instinctual demands of the id and the conscientious demands of the super-ego" (*SE,* 23:172–73).

The Oedipus Complex Revisited

I want to consider briefly two other aspects of Freud's rethinking of the Oedipus complex in the context of the structural theory and then make a few comments on its present status. My first subject is what Freud calls the complete Oedipus complex. The complete Oedipus complex is both positive and negative and is "due to the bisexuality originally present in children." Thus, a boy has an ambivalent attitude toward his father and an affectionate attitude toward his mother (the positive complex) but also an affectionate attitude toward his father and an ambivalent attitude toward his mother (the negative complex). For the girl there is a similar twofold complex (though Freud leaves this unstated): an ambivalent attitude toward the mother and an affectionate attitude toward the father and an affectionate attitude toward the mother and an ambivalent attitude toward the father. The superego, then, represents an identification for boy and girl with both parents, its relative intensity reflecting the "preponderance" of the two sexual dispositions (*SE,* 19:33–34).[15]

Having defined identification as occurring only after the giving up of a sexual object, Freud evidently needs the complete Oedipus complex to explain the child's identification with the same-sexed parent. Aside from this theoretical need, Simon and Blass argue, "there does not seem to be any evidence compelling the postulation of parallel inverse triadic relationships." The idea of a universal mother-son rivalry for the father, they continue, is "not intuitively obvious, clinical data supporting it are not forthcoming, and even a hypothetical description of such a rivalry is not presented by Freud or his analytic colleagues" (Simon and Blass, 167). Significantly, Freud's description of the Oedipus complex in *An Outline of Psycho-Analysis* contains only a passing reference to the complete Oedipus complex (*SE,* 23:187–94).

My second subject is Freud's version of the female Oedipus complex, which he now understands is not simply analogous to the boy's. He begins to describe the difference in "The Dissolution of the Oedipus Complex" and continues to refine the difference in a series of three essays: "Some Psychical Consequences of the Anatomical Distinction between the Sexes" (1925); "Female Sexuality" (1931); and the chapter on "Femininity" in *New Introductory Lectures on Psycho-Analysis* (1933). Consistent with his position in *Three Essays,* Freud views feminine sexuality in terms of libidinal development. Both boy and girl enter the phallic stage in the same masculine mode—the boy deriving "pleasurable sensations" from his penis, the girl from her clitoris. The "truly feminine vagina" is undiscovered by both. But with the advent of puberty the "clitoris should wholly or in part hand over its sensitivity . . . to the vagina." Unlike the boy, then, the girl must abandon her original infantile erotogenic zone—one of two tasks she must perform in her development (*SE,* 22:118).

The second task is the abandonment of her attachment to her mother, who is the first sexual object for both the girl and the boy. But in the Oedipus situation the girl must turn to her father as a love object, while the boy continues in his primary object cathexis of the mother (118–21).

What interests Freud about this second task is that the girl's attachment to the mother ends, not simply with a change of object, but with a hostility to the mother that may last for a lifetime. He considers a number of reasons for the girl's reproaches against her mother—that she gave too little milk, that she bore another child, that she forbade pleasurable genital activity—but concludes that these sources of reproach also operate in the boy (122–24).

Freud finds the specific source of the girl's reproaches against her mother in the castration complex. Noting her lack of a penis, she holds her mother responsible for this lack and does not forgive her for it. From penis envy—the content of her castration complex—she must move toward normal femininity by abandoning her mother as a sexual object and turning toward her father as an object of affection. Originally she turns to the father with a wish for the penis. With the substitution of the wish for a penis with a wish for a penis-baby from her father, the girl enters the Oedipus complex. Thus, as Freud says, for a girl the castration complex prepares for the Oedipus complex, whereas for a boy it leads to a repression of the complex. In girls the chief motive for leaving the Oedipus complex is absent. They remain in it for an indeterminate time, and they leave it late and incompletely. The result is a superego of less strength and independence—hence of less cultural significance—than in boys (124–29).

From the time of their first appearance, Freud's ideas on female development aroused controversy. Freud may have thought that he was simply working out certain theoretical views, but he also knew that what he said would cause debate and disagreement. Within psychoanalysis this debate centered on the idea of penis envy—not its existence, as might be supposed, but how to interpret it. As Gay says, "dissenters like Karen Horney and Ernest Jones concentrated on woman's nature and refused acquiescence in Freud's formula that femininity is essentially acquired by the successive renunciation of masculine traits." Horney placed penis envy in a "context of normal female development" (Gay 1988, 519). She argues that the girl loves the father because of a biologically grounded heterosexual attraction to the father based on a primary identification with the mother. Horney further asserts that Freud's theory of femininity is identical to the ideas a boy has of a girl. For her, as Appignanesi and Forrester say, male analysts were themselves stuck "in the little boy's phallic phase, dominated by the division of the world into beings possessing a penis and beings who are castrated"—a view also held by many contemporary feminists who see Freud as the spokesman for a masculine culture (Appignanesi and Forrester, 437). In addition to penis envy, other aspects of Freud's theory of feminine development—the masochism and narcissism of women, the shift from clitoral to vaginal sexuality, and the weak superego—have been challenged both by psychoanalysts and feminists, who continue to disagree with Freud's version of the girl's Oedipus complex.[16]

There is also much disagreement about the nature and importance of the Oedipus complex for both boys and girls. For Freud it is the nuclear complex of the neuroses and the crucial stage in normal development. Before Freud's death (in the work of Melanie Klein) and continuing thereafter, psychoanalysts increasingly turned to a study of the pre-Oedipal period, which Freud had only briefly described in the essays on the feminine. This interest led to a focus on the mother-child dyad rather than the Oedipal triad. It also led to a study of such developmental issues as mother-infant attachment, separation-individuation, and the origin and nature of selfhood. For many clinicians, as Simon and Blass observe, the crucial phases in the development of psychopathology and character are those preceding the emergence of the Oedipus complex. Its clinical centrality is thus diminished for such analysts.

But the complex has not disappeared. According to Simon and Blass, however, it has been considerably transformed from Freud's version. They report the following consensus (not unanimity) as to what is enduring in Freud's formulations: the child has complex relationships with both parents; these relationships have a developmental history; and the child loves and hates both parents, wants to be like them, fears them, at times uses one parent to gain something from the other, and expresses sexual feelings and fantasies, which change according to family and cultural pressures, toward the parents. In addition, because the parents were once children "there are complex reverberations between the feelings of the child and residual childhood feelings of the parents." Anything beyond this minimal description, Simon and Blass say, cannot be justified by conclusive evidence that supports either detailed clinical propositions or sweeping generalizations (such as the innateness and universality of the complex) (Simon and Blass, 173).[17] Interestingly, the consensus they describe seems very close to the view of rivalry and competition in the family proposed by parent-offspring conflict theory, which is usually seen by its proponents as a replacement for Freud's Oedipal theory.[18]

The Theory of Anxiety

Inhibitions, Symptoms, and Anxiety is a result of Freud's increased interest in the ego. In this book Freud alters an understanding of anxiety he has held since the 1890s—that anxiety is caused by undischarged libido (as in anxiety neurosis). But this concept of anxiety leaves Freud with two seemingly unrelated kinds of anxiety—neurotic and realistic (anxiety about a perceived external danger)—which have the same physiological and subjective characteristics and hence must be related. In *Introductory Lectures on Psycho-Analysis* he tries to bring them together but only by unconvincingly arguing that the realistic anxiety that apparently comes from the ego instincts really comes from the ego libido (*SE,* 16:430).

Now, in light of the structural theory and the role of the castration complex, Freud is able to correlate neurotic with realistic anxiety. Reviewing the animal phobias of Little Hans and the Wolf Man, he now argues that the affect of anxiety (the essence of a phobia) comes "not from the libidinal cathexes of the repressed impulses, but from the repressing agency itself"—that is, from the ego. As an "untransformed fear of castration," this anxiety is realistic—"a fear of a danger which was actually impending or was judged to be a real one." So, he concludes, it is "anxiety which produced repression and not, as I formerly believed, repression which produced anxiety" (*SE,* 20:108–9). As an affective signal of danger, the anxiety aroused internally "differs in no respect from the realistic anxiety which the ego normally feels in situations of danger, except that its content remains unconscious and only becomes conscious in the form of a distortion" (126).[19]

Having identified signal anxiety as an ego function, Freud now wants to understand what anxiety really is. Structurally, he says, anxiety is a state of unpleasure "with acts of discharge along particular paths" (133). The prototype of discharge along particular paths is the experience of birth, which, though it has no psychological content, is an event in which "large sums of excitation" crowd upon the newborn and produce feelings of unpleasure. So the baby "will repeat its affect of anxiety in every situation which recalls the event of birth" (135). But this experience of birth, Freud insists, produces only a preparedness for anxiety, which increases as mental development occurs and lasts "over a certain period of childhood" (136).[20] The question then becomes, What situations recall the event of birth and what is it that is recalled? These two questions lead back to the function of anxiety as a reaction to danger.

Birth, Freud thinks, is a danger, but not in a psychological sense. The newborn can only perceive large sums of excitation that produce feelings of unpleasure. What Freud means is that only the physiology of anxiety (increased heart and respiratory rate, dyspnea, sweating, tremor, and muscle tension) is prefigured by the experience of birth. Psychological anxiety requires the development of an awareness of danger situations, of which he identifies three for the child: fear of the loss of a loved object, fear of castration, and fear of the superego. Like birth, each of these dangers involves a separation—from the mother, from the penis, from the love of the superego (136–40).

But these external dangers are not the whole story. As Freud makes clear, there are also internal forces at work. Thus, the infant wants to keep the mother's love because she satisfies all its needs. The real danger is a nonsatisfaction of these needs and a growing tension against which it is helpless. The infant experiences this accumulating stimulation that cannot be mastered or discharged as analogous to the danger of birth, and this experience leads to an anxiety reaction. In other words, the infant fears the absence of the mother because she is the person who "satisfies all its needs without delay" (137). In castration anxiety, the same instinctual need is present. Being deprived of the penis means the impossibility of being united with the mother (or a substitute for her), and this in turn "means being helplessly exposed to an unpleasurable tension due to instinctual need, as was the case at birth" (139). Anxiety is no longer the result of transformed libido, and real external dangers are involved in its generation. But the principle of tension reduction remains very much at the center of Freud's revised theory of anxiety.

Each type of anxiety is phase specific. In early infancy the individual is not able to master large sums of internal and external excitation. Later the individual's "most important interest really is that the people he is dependent on should not withdraw their loving care of him" (146). In boyhood, aware of his "sexual intentions toward his mother" and his aggressive feelings toward his father, "he really is justified in being afraid of his father" (146–47). Finally, as he enters into social relationships, he must fear his superego, for its absence "would give rise to severe conflicts, dangers, and so on" (147).

What continues to puzzle Freud is why these early dangers should persist into later life when the individual is fully capable of mastering stimuli, of satisfying his own needs, and of realizing that castration is no longer a danger. This persistence is, he thinks, precisely the case for those who become neurotic as adults. As he says, "a great many people remain infantile in their behaviour in regard to danger and do not overcome determinants of anxiety which have grown out of date" (148). Why, he asks, does anxiety evoke reactions that are abnormal and that "run counter to the movement of life?" But he has no answer to this riddle of neurosis. "After tens of years of psychoanalytic labours," he concludes, "we are as much in the dark about this problem as we were at the start" (148–49).

But if the ultimate reason for neurosis is unclear, the role of anxiety in symptom formation is not. Anxiety signals to the ego the presence of an internal (instinctual) danger. This anxiety leads to symptom formation by giving the ego the power to "arrest the process which is beginning in the id and which threatens danger." To master this internal danger, the ego makes use of the mechanisms of defense (of which repression is only one)—a defensive process that attempts flight from an instinctual danger just as one would flee an external danger. Symptom formation ends this danger situation by turning the id impulse into a substitutive formation and also tries to bind the anxiety generated by the danger situation (144–45). Thus, even in the structural view, a symptom is still a compromise formation between id impulse and ego defense. After the Oedipal period, of course, the superego is a factor in defense.

Technique Revisited

The two 1937 essays, "Analysis Terminable and Interminable" and "Constructions in Analysis," are the last strictly psychoanalytic works published during Freud's lifetime. Both continue to be important sources of ideas and debate among contemporary psychoanalysts.[21]

"Analysis Terminable and Interminable" is notable for its emphasis on the limitations of analytic treatment. In accounting for these limitations, Freud stresses the constitutional strength of the instincts (either at birth or during such life periods as puberty or menopause when the instincts are reinforced), alterations of the ego that result from the need for defense and that appear in analysis as a resistance against recovery, and the death instinct (*SE,* 23:224–30, 234–40, 242–47). Only for acquired or traumatic neuroses does Freud appear optimistic in this essay (220). Where there is a constitutional strength of instinct and an "unfavorable" alteration of the ego, the analysis is restricted in effectiveness and may be "interminable" (220–21). By his own admission never a therapeutic enthusiast, Freud here proposes a very modest goal. "The business of the analysis," he says, "is to secure the best possible psychological conditions for the functions of the ego; with that it has discharged its task" (250). Apparently these conditions generate neither permanent cure nor prophylaxis against a different neurotic problem—though, if life and fate are kind, they might.

In "Constructions in Analysis" Freud addresses the issue of how the analyst constructs or reconstructs the patient's past. Ellman suggests that Freud is attempting to remind analysts of the importance of remembering, especially those who had recently argued that only the transference can be analyzed (Ellman, 222–23). Freud is also trying to state criteria for determining the adequacy and the accuracy of constructions.

Whereas an interpretation is the analyst's reading of a single element of material (such as a parapraxis), a construction is the analyst's picture of a forgotten piece of the patient's early history (*SE,* 23:259). Since a patient's yes or no to an analyst's construction cannot be taken at face value, how is the construction to be confirmed? Only indirectly, Freud says, though he insists that such confirmation is "in every respect trustworthy." So, for example, the patient might respond to a proposed construction by saying something like " 'I didn't ever think . . . that,' " which Freud argues can be translated as " 'Yes, you're right this time—about my *unconscious.*' " Or the patient might answer with an association "which contains something similar or analogous to the content of the construction" (263; Freud's italics). Finally, in an analysis dominated by a sense of guilt or a masochistic need to suffer, a correct construction causes an aggravation of symptoms (265). The trouble is that the analyst's construction does not always end in the patient's recollections. In such cases, Freud says, "we produce in him an assured conviction of the truth of the construction which achieves the same therapeutic result as a recaptured memory" (266).

It's unfortunate that Freud saves for a later inquiry (never written) a description of how this assured conviction occurs. As it stands, his statement does not preclude suggestion on the part of the analyst, in spite of his assertion that such an abuse of suggestion has never occurred in his practice and that it is "enormously exaggerated" as a factor in analysis (262). Nor does it preclude the view that Freud imposes on his patients constructions that support his own theoretical or personal preoccupations. For example, the Wolf Man's primal scene may be Freud's construction of an event necessary for the refutation of Jung and Adler, not a memory of the patient's.[22] Reconstruction, as Spence says, is "clearly a creative enterprise whose form depends on the goals in question. What 'really happened' has many different faces and can be told from many points of view." In this "unpacking" the "motives and goals of the unpacker are playing a significant part in what is selected" (Spence 1987, 103). Like the question of the therapeutic effectiveness of psychoanalysis, the problem of the truth of Freud's or any psychoanalyst's construction is presently highly controversial and likely to remain so for some time.[23]

Suggestion is not the only issue in this controversy. The nature of memory is also involved. Is memory, as Spence argues, always only a narrative truth created by the analyst and the patient? Or does memory, even if distorted, sometimes point to a real historical truth about the personal past of the patient? In spite of having apparently abandoned the idea of memory as historical in moving from literal seduction to fantasies of seduction, Freud continues to look for the reality (or the partial reality) behind the patient's associations. So do many contemporary psychoanalysts and memory researchers. But the issue is far from settled.[24]

On Religion and Culture

In a 1935 postscript to *An Autobiographical Study,* Freud writes of his intellectual alteration after 1923. "My interest," he says, "after making a lifelong *détour* through the natural sciences, medicine and psychotherapy, returned to the cultural problems which had fascinated me long before, when I was a youth scarcely old enough for thinking" (*SE,* 20:72). The result of this alteration over the next 16 years was three of Freud's best-known and most widely read books.

The Future of an Illusion is Freud's most sustained and rationalist attack on religion—hardly surprising for a lifelong atheist. The Freud of this book belongs to the antimetaphysical, anticlerical, antidogmatic position of such eighteenth-century *philosophes* as Voltaire and Diderot or of the nineteenth-century critic of religion Ludwig Feuerbach (1804–1872), whose work he read as a young man (*Freud-Silberstein,* 70, 96). Freud claims nothing new in his argument except to add "some psychological foundation" to previous rationalist critiques of religion (*SE,* 21:35).

For Freud, the dogmas of religion are illusions, "fulfilments of the oldest, strongest and most urgent wishes of mankind." The secret of their strength "lies in the strength of those wishes" (30). Religion arises from the helplessness of humankind—of the child in relation to the parents, of early man in relation to nature, and of all people in relation to the sufferings brought on them by others. So the gods have a threefold task: they must "exorcise the terrors of nature," they must reconcile men to the cruelty of fate (especially death), and they must compensate for the sufferings and privation of civilized life. Religion, then, is "born from man's need to make his helplessness tolerable and built up from the material of memories of the helplessness of his own childhood and the childhood of the human race" (18). Naturally, man's gods are merely the figure of the all-powerful father of childhood or the all-powerful primal father writ large—a figure dreaded, in need of propitiation, yet entrusted as a protector.

It is time, Freud thinks, for humankind to outgrow religion. Just as children outgrow the obsessive neurosis of childhood, so human beings can outgrow religion, the "universal obsessional neurosis of humanity" (43).[25] What will replace it, he argues, is science. With people freed from the illusion of religion and from a morality and education based on it, it might be possible through science to gain a realistic knowledge of the world, to increase human powers, and to develop "rational grounds for the precepts of civilization" (44).[26]

But Freud's optimism about being reconciled to civilization does not last long.[27] Three years later in *Civilization and Its Discontents* it is gone. This may seem like a sudden change, but it isn't really. For one thing, Freud had never been an optimist about either human nature or the purpose of civilization. In his own mind he was always neither an optimist nor a pessimist, merely a realist. Then, of course, there is his long-held view that civilization is based on instinctual renunciation, which produces frustration and a hostility to civilization. Finally, by 1930 he has thought through the implication of describing the superego as a pure culture of the death instinct. These personal and theoretical ideas, in combination with the Austrian and German political situation of the 1920s and his experience of the misery and destruction of World War I, would seem to explain the difference in tone between the two books.

As a starting point, Freud assumes that individuals seek happiness, which is twofold: a strong feeling of pleasure and the absence of pain and unpleasure. He thus continues to see the pleasure principle as the main motive force in human behavior. Positive pleasure, he thinks, is impossible to achieve except momentarily, for people's happiness seems not to be the intention of creation. Unhappiness is much easier to experience and comes from three sources: our own body, the external world, and our relations with other people (the most painful source of suffering of the three). About the first two, little can be done (except, as Freud shows in *The Future of an Illusion,* the consolation of religion). But with the third, "we cannot see why the regulations made by ourselves should not, on the contrary, be a protection and a benefit for every one of us." Perhaps, he suggests, a piece of "unconquerable nature" is at work here—"this time a piece of our own psychical constitution." Maybe our civilization is largely responsible for our misery and we "should be much happier if we gave it up and returned to primitive conditions" (*SE,* 21:86).

In *Group Psychology* Freud saw an aim-inhibited love (in *Beyond the Pleasure Principle,* Eros) binding ever larger numbers of people into a community. Now, in *Civilization and Its Discontents,* Freud asks why Eros (in cooperation with the compulsion to work created by the external world) does not ensure the further development of civilization "smoothly towards an even better control over the external world and towards a further extension of the number of people included in the community" (101)? As for work, Freud thinks most people are averse to it (80 n). There are two problems with love. First, love comes into "opposition to the interests of civilization." Second, "civilization threatens love with substantial restrictions" (103).

Love opposes civilization in the opposition between the family and the larger community. Civilization wants to bring people together in large unities. The family refuses to give up the individual. Sexual love, moreover, is a relationship between "two individuals in which a third can only be superfluous or disturbing" (108). Civilization, Freud insists, is not content with a community of libidinally connected double individuals. In order to summon up aim-inhibited libido on the scale necessary to bind large numbers together, "a restriction upon sexual life is unavoidable" (109).

In addressing the question of why civilization thus restricts love with coercion and harsh morality, Freud arrives at his true subject in *Civilization and Its Discontents.* There must, he thinks, be some "disturbing factor" here that he has not yet discovered (109). That factor is aggression. Human beings, Freud says, are not gentle creatures who want love. They are creatures among whose "instinctual endowments is to be reckoned a powerful share of aggressiveness" (111). Aggression, of course, is the death instinct directed toward objects in the external world. It is "an original, self-subsisting instinctual disposition in man" and "constitutes the greatest impediment to civilization." It opposes the progress of Eros in combining individuals into the "unity of mankind." Thus, the evolution of civilization presents the struggle between Eros and the death instinct. No wonder civilization needs aim-inhibited libido in such quantities that it increasingly restricts the sexual instincts. Only Eros can oppose the death instinct in the struggle for the "life of the human species" (122).

The most important method by which civilization inhibits aggression is to internalize it, to direct it back toward the ego, where it is taken over by the superego, which is prepared to direct this aggression against the ego.[28] The tension between ego and superego produces a sense of guilt, which "expresses itself as a need for punishment" (123). So civilization masters aggression by setting up an agency in the individual to "watch over it, like a garrison in a conquered city" (124).

Freud's discussion of aggression and guilt in the last two chapters of *Civilization and Its Discontents* is elaborate and complicated, and I will present only its main elements. First, the sense of guilt has two origins. One is the fear of an authority, who insists upon instinctual renunciation. The other is an internalizing of this authority (the father, say) as the superego, which demands both instinctual renunciation as well as punishment "since the continuance of the forbidden wishes cannot be concealed from the super-ego" (127). For the superego, even the wish to satisfy an instinct requires punishment. Thus, even saints rightly call themselves sinners, for "temptations are merely increased by constant frustration" (126).

Second, Freud associates a sense of guilt only with a frustration of the aggressive, not the libidinal, instincts (138). What begins as the aggressive imposition of parental authority against instinctual satisfaction (including inhibition of the satisfaction of the aggressive impulse being directed at the prohibiting authority) is internalized as self-aggression (the initial state of the death instinct). The aggressiveness of conscience continues the aggressiveness of the external authority. At first, conscience forces the renunciation of aggression. But every fresh renunciation of aggression "is taken over by the super-ego and increases the latter's aggressiveness (against the ego)" (129). Thus conscience increases in "severity and intolerance" (128). It is truly a pure culture of the death instinct. This vicious cycle may produce heights of guilt "that the individual finds hard to tolerate" (133). As Freud says, his intention is to represent the "sense of guilt as the most important problem in the development of civilization and to show that the price we pay for our advance in civilization is a loss of happiness through the heightening of the sense of guilt" (134). Though often not perceived as such, this guilt may remain unconscious and appear as a sort of malaise or unrest in civilization (135–36).[29] Freud doesn't say so, but clearly an intolerable sense of guilt may lead to outbreaks of external aggression in an individual who is trying to avert self-destruction.[30]

Third, the severity of the superego may not correspond to the severity of the child's upbringing. A child leniently brought up may have a severe conscience. An unduly lenient father causes an overstrict superego because the child cannot express aggression against a loving father and so turns his aggression inward. The end result is no different from the suppression and internalizing of aggression directed at a stern father. As is usual with Freud, innate constitution (quantity of aggression) and influences from the environment "act in combination" (130). No upbringing (except for delinquents, who have received no love and who can direct their aggression externally) offers escape from the development of a sense of guilt. As Freud never tires of saying, since human beings are biologically committed to a long period of dependence on loved caretakers, the sense of guilt—like the Oedipus complex of which it is the heir—is inescapable.

The case of the loving father leads to a final point. Though guilt results from the renunciation of aggression, love is implicated in its genesis. In both the murder of the primal father (to which Freud refers) and the child's hostility to his prohibiting parents, there is always ambivalence. Because ambivalence means love as well as hate, it makes no difference whether one has killed one's father or only wishes to. Guilt results in either case, for loving the father leads to an identification with him that sets up the superego as a punishment against the real or intended deed. In a widened community the same conflict continues, is strengthened, and results in increased guilt. Thus civilization, which "obeys an internal erotic impulsion which causes human beings to unite in a closely-knit group," can only "achieve this aim through an ever-increasing reinforcement of the sense of guilt" (132–33).

For Freud, then, the "fateful question" for humanity is whether and to what extent cultural development will succeed in mastering the "instinct of aggression and self-destruction." It is hard to see from Freud's analysis how such mastery is to occur. In fact, there is a tragic impasse in his position: only in a state of nature is there no instinctual renunciation, but there is also a war of all against all; in civilization there is an increasing sense of guilt that may well explode outward at any time. The problem of the unrest in culture is especially pressing at a time when men have the means to exterminate each other "to the last man." Freud offers neither consolation nor despair, merely the hope that "eternal Eros" will assert himself in the struggle with the death instinct (145).[31]

Freud and Moses

Freud wrote the first draft of *Moses and Monotheism* in the summer of 1934. Its original title was *The Man Moses, An Historical Novel.* In the same letter to Arnold Zweig in which he mentions this title, Freud refers to this book as falling into three sections—the first "like an interesting novel," the second "laborious and boring," and the third involving a "theory of religion."[32] The first two essays appeared in the journal *Imago* in 1937, but the third one continued to give him trouble and did not appear in print until the three essays were published in book form in 1939. Some of the trouble, as he tells Zweig, is his fear of a bias against psychoanalysis in Catholic Vienna that would affect the livelihood of all the psychoanalysts in the city (*Freud-Zweig,* 92). Only in England after the German invasion, as he says in a second prefatory note to the third essay, does he now feel free to publish this essay (*SE,* 23:57).

Freud's preoccupation with Moses was lifelong. It was never simply intellectual but always deeply personal, for some of his biographers nothing short of an identification—that is, Moses is to the Jewish religion as Freud is to psychoanalysis.[33] Even in "The Moses of Michelangelo" (1914), which is ostensibly an analysis of Michelangelo's statue, it is clear that Freud identifies with Moses in controlling his anger against the faithless Jews (that is, the defectors Jung and Adler).

But Freud has an immediate reason for turning again to the subject of Moses in 1934. As he says to Zweig, "Faced with the new persecutions, one asks oneself how the Jews have come to be what they are and why they have attracted this undying hatred. I soon discovered the formula: Moses created the Jews" (*Freud-Zweig,* 91). Freud's famous (or infamous) identification of Moses as an Egyptian rather than a Jew is for him "not the essential point, though it is the starting point" (*Freud-Zweig,* 91, 98). The essential point, as Yerushalmi says, in the context of Hitler and the Nazis is the "question of what it means to be a Jew"—no doubt the "immediate impulse to the actual writing of *Moses and Monotheism*" (Yerushalmi, 15).[34]

Nevertheless, he does start by claiming that Moses has an Egyptian name (a fact long recognized) because he is an Egyptian. This is not an entirely new idea for, as Yerushalmi observes, the "Egyptian descent of Moses is itself no novelty"—many contemporary and ancient writers had already suggested this possibility (Yerushalmi, 5). In Freud's version of this idea, Moses is not only an Egyptian but an aristocratic Egyptian, possibly a member of the royal house and an adherent of the monotheism of Amenophis IV (Akhenaten). After this pharaoh's death and the suppression of the monotheism he had attempted to force on the polytheistic Egyptians, Moses is left without a country or a religion. He chooses a Semitic tribe then living in Egypt "to be his people," becomes their leader, and leads them out of Egypt "peacefully and unpursued" (*SE,* 23:28–29). He brings with him the monotheism of the dead pharaoh with its "highly spiritualized notion of god, the idea of a single deity embracing the whole world, who was not less all-loving than all-powerful, who was averse to all ceremonial and magic and set before men as their highest aim a life in truth and justice" (50). He also brings circumcision, a rule against pictorial representation of any kind, and a rejection of the idea of an afterlife.

Sometime after the Exodus the Jews rose against their leader, killed him, abandoned the religion he had imposed on them, and repressed the murder. Two generations or a century later, they joined with other Semites in Midian and adopted their "coarse, narrow-minded . . . violent and bloodthirsty" local volcanic god, Yahweh (50). So the god of Moses and Yahweh were fused, and Moses became identified with a Midianite priest also called Moses. For Freud, then, there were two Moseses. But the religion of the first Moses survived over the centuries through the efforts of the prophets who "tirelessly preached the old Mosaic doctrine" (51). Finally, the god of the Jews became like the god of the original Moses: he was the only god; he despised ceremonial and sacrifice and wanted only a life of truth and justice. The murder of the first Moses, however, remained repressed.[35]

Clearly, this is a version of the primal horde murder occurring in historical time. So Freud bases the murder of Moses on a supposed historical fact—the 1922 hypothesis of Ernst Sellin that the book of *Hosea* contains a hidden memory of this murder—a view held by no one and later repudiated by Sellin, as Freud knew (Jones 1957, 3:373).[36] Freud is nothing if not stubborn. He was undeterred by this information.

After all, he needs the murder of Moses to establish the analogy with the primal murder of *Totem and Taboo*—not, this time, to study the beginning of civilization but to study the continued evolution of religion from its origins in totemism into historical time. As is apparent in part 3 of *Moses and Monotheism,* "Moses, His People, and Monotheist Religion," that is one of his primary goals. The murder of Moses is a repetition of the primal murder. Like the earlier murder, this one inaugurates a new cycle of religious belief, albeit at a level very far advanced over totemism. Like an individual neurosis (obsessional, of course), this cycle follows a pattern of early trauma (the murder of Moses)—defense (repression of the murder and abandonment of his religion)—latency (the period of Yahweh worship and covert Mosaic tradition)—and partial return of the repressed (renewed obedience to the first Moses but with the murder suppressed). Only with Christianity's acknowledgment of the murder of the father does the repressed fully return (though the crime is still distorted by the shadowy concept of original sin).

The Mosaic religion does not survive during the latency period by tradition based on communication, for such a tradition would lack the "compulsive character that attaches to religious phenomena" (*SE,* 23:101). As a repetition of the murder of the primal father, the murder of Moses activates inherited "memory-traces of the experience of our ancestors" and leads to the "re-establishment of the primal father in his historic rights" (99, 86). Thus Freud's position in *Moses and Monotheism* is based entirely on the inheritance of acquired characteristics with all the problems (of which he is fully aware) of that concept (100). Given the centrality of this hypothesis for his argument and the purely speculative nature of the idea of the murder of Moses, it is not surprising that Biblical scholars have dismissed *Moses and Monotheism* as a work of historical scholarship.

In addition to a historical reconstruction of the origins of the Jewish religion, there are two other related themes in part 3 of this book. One is the roots of anti-Semitism. He finds these roots of hostility to the Jews in several sources: in their minority existence among other people; in their indefinable difference from their host nations; in their defiance of oppression; in their capacity for success in commercial and cultural activity; in the jealousy aroused by their claims to be the favorite child of God; in their custom of circumcision, which recalls castration; and in the hatred of Christianity by Christians whose ancestors were polytheists and who displace their hatred onto the Jews (90–91).

The second of these two themes is Freud's attempt to describe the essence of the Jewish religion. Freud is explicit on this essence: it lies in what he calls the advance in intellectuality.[37] The Mosaic prohibition meant that "a sensory perception was given second place to what may be called an abstract idea—a triumph of intellectuality over sensuality" (113). This "dematerialization" of God had a profound effect on the Jewish people, who "retained their inclination to intellectual interests"

(115). Even Christianity, which represents an advance over Judaism in the return of the repressed, did not maintain the high intellectual level of the Jews, for it diluted a pure monotheism with the rituals of surrounding people, a mother goddess, and other thinly disguised divinities of polytheism, and it did not exclude superstition, magic, and mysticism (88). Jewish monotheism, then, represents an instinctual renunciation of immense importance for the future of civilization. As Freud says to Albert Einstein in "Why War" (1933), a "strengthening of the intellect, which is beginning to govern instinctual life" is one of the two most important psychological characteristics of civilization, the other being the internalization of aggression (*SE,* 22:214–15). What Freud seems to suggest here and in *Moses and Monotheism* is that the process of civilization may be moving toward the replacement of instinct by intellect. If so, Jewish monotheism is an important stage in this process. Maybe it is even worth the fate of persecution.

Chapter Six
Epilogue

In *Revolution in Science,* Bernard Cohen says that the three greatest intellectual revolutions of the past century "are associated with the names of Karl Marx, Charles Darwin, and Sigmund Freud."[1] In terms of intellectual revolutions and influence, this statement is unexceptionable. The simplest measure of its truth as regards Freud is the widespread popular dissemination of Freudian ideas (however distorted and misunderstood) in the West, if not the world. Everyone knows what Freudian means, even if very few actually know what Freudian really means. Few people—even artists, politicians, and performers—achieve the kind of (seemingly) permanent grassroots currency of Freud. It may even be that this is the profoundest influence any one person can have on his or her culture.

But Freud's influence extends beyond the domain of popular culture. His ideas have influenced many people in all aspects of modern culture—drama, poetry, fiction, painting, film, history, philosophy, anthropology, and even theology. All mental health professionals who practice some form of the talking cure—as well as the millions of people involved in such therapy—are indebted to Freud, even when they no longer think of themselves as Freudian or even actively repudiate Freud's ideas. So Cohen doesn't exaggerate in naming Freud as one of the makers of the modern world.

Cohen, however, isn't really interested in cultural revolutions. As the title of his book suggests, he is interested in scientific revolutions. There, as he admits, the Freudian revolution is ambiguous because there is no agreement on its status as science. "Is Freudian psychoanalysis," he asks, "science, or is it social science, or is it not even science at all?" (Cohen, 352). Freud thought of himself as a scientist and of psychoanalysis as a natural science—a natural science of the unconscious. So Cohen raises an important question—maybe the most important question about Freud and psychoanalysis in the 1990s. Many critics of Freud through this century—and especially current ones—do not doubt the answer. For them Freudian psychoanalysis is not a science at all—by which, as

Flanagan says, they do not mean it is more like the arts than physics or chemistry but that it is "intellectual gobbledygook—pure, unadulterated, but undeniably seductive nonsense" (Flanagan, 74). For these critics Freud is a rhetorician who, by repeated verbal sleights of hand, compels belief in ideas that in fact have no empirical basis. Others view the nonscientific status of Freud's ideas as a virtue and link them to the social sciences or (as in much hermeneutic psychoanalysis) to history. As a historical, hermeneutic enterprise, they argue, psychoanalysis studies human meaning and intention, reasons rather than causes, and its aim is to construct a coherent life narrative that is therapeutic.[2]

In spite of the claim that psychoanalysis is a seductive mirage or, at best, a hermeneutic discipline, the issue of its scientific status remains very much alive. But questions as to what kind of science it is and what criteria are to be used to evaluate its various concepts and hypotheses—some of which may be correct, some incorrect—vary widely.[3] Not surprisingly, many claim that only the approved method of quantitative, experimentally controlled observation by a neutral observer will do. Many others disagree that a positivist, experimental model is appropriate for the study of human subjectivity and meaning. Frosh, for example, suggests that scientific activity in the social and humanistic sciences is better "regarded as a systematic collection of evidence using transparent means (that is, methods available to scrutiny) and tolerating the possibility of alternative explanations to those promoted by any particular theory" (Frosh, 40). Forrester argues that psychoanalysis is "continuous with ordinary everyday explanations" and that psychoanalytic explanations should be "judged on roughly the same criteria as we judge everyday non-psychoanalytic explanations" (Forrester, 242). Lear proposes that Freud stands at the beginning of a new science of subjectivity and that "we do not have any fixed model to which it should conform" (Lear, 6). Still others—such as Eagle, Bucci, Slavin and Kriegman, and Laurence Miller—think that psychoanalysis can become more scientific by opening itself to such empirically based disciplines as cognitive theory, evolutionary psychology, developmental psychology, and neuroscience.[4]

I have no ready answer as to the outcome of the debate on the scientific standing of Freud and psychoanalysis. It seems unlikely that this debate will end any time soon. It seems likely that it will continue to be acrimonious and uncivil, in which respect the century will end as it began. It also seems likely that this debate, in combination with the proliferation of new psychoanalytic models, will reinforce and hasten the continued modification, reformulation, or supersession of many of Freud's original concepts.[5] For the Freud who expected psychoanalysis to be replaced by an adequate neuroscience, this is surely the way science should work.

Notes and References

Chapter One

1. Sigismund occurs four times in 1874 and once in 1875. Thereafter he used only Sigmund. *The Letters of Sigmund Freud to Eduard Silberstein, 1871–1881,* ed. Walter Boehlich, trans. Arnold J. Pomerans (Cambridge: Belknap Press of Harvard University Press, 1990); hereafter cited in text as *Freud-Silberstein.*

2. This is Freud's own account in *An Autobiographical Study (1925).* See *The Standard Edition of the Complete Psychological Works of Sigmund Freud,* 24 vols., translated from the German under the general editorship of James Strachey in collaboration with Anna Freud, assisted by Alix Strachey and Alan Tyson (London: Hogarth Press, 1955–1974), 20:8; hereafter cited in text as *SE,* followed by volume and page numbers.

3. Marianne Krüll, *Freud and His Father,* trans. Arnold J. Pomerans (New York: Norton, 1986), 85; hereafter cited in text.

4. Yosef Hayim Yerushalmi, *Freud's Moses: Judaism Terminable and Interminable* (New Haven and London: Yale University Press, 1991), 64–70; hereafter cited in text. Yerushalmi takes exception to Krüll's portrait of the Freud family as a completely liberalized and enlightened family and to her acceptance of Freud's public assertion of his non-Jewish education. On Freud and the Philippson Bible, see William J. McGrath, *Freud's Discovery of Psychoanalysis: The Politics of Hysteria* (Ithaca and London: Cornell University Press, 1986), 44–58; hereafter cited in text.

5. *Letters of Sigmund Freud,* selected and edited by Ernst L. Freud and translated by Tania and James Stern (New York: Basic Books, 1960), 366; hereafter cited in text as *Letters.* This quotation is from a letter of 6 May 1926 to the members of the B'Nai B'Brith Lodge of which Freud had been a member since 1897.

6. The phrase "compact majority" is from Henrik Ibsen's *An Enemy of the People.* For a fuller discussion of Freud as a Jew, see also Peter Gay, *A Godless Jew: Freud, Atheism, and the Making of Psychoanalysis* (New Haven and London: Yale University Press, 1987), esp. 117–54; hereafter cited in text. For a brief summary of the competing views on the nature and importance of Freud's Jewishness, see Ivan Oxaal, "The Jewish Origins of Psychoanalysis Reconsidered," in *Freud in Exile: Psychoanalysis and Its Vicissitudes,* ed. Edward Timms and Naomi Segal (New Haven and London: Yale University Press, 1988), 37–53.

7. Martin Freud, *Sigmund Freud: Man and Father* (New York: Vanguard Press, 1958), 19.

8. For a full discussion of Jacob's financial situation and the leaving of Freiberg, see Krüll, 143–47.

9. *The Complete Letters of Sigmund Freud to Wilhelm Fliess, 1887–1904,* trans. and ed. Jeffrey Moussaieff Masson (Cambridge: Belknap Press of Harvard University Press, 1985), 202; hereafter cited in text as *Freud-Fliess.*

10. Peter Gay, *Freud: A Life for Our Times* (New York: Norton, 1988), 11; hereafter cited in text.

11. Deborah P. Margolis, *Freud and His Mother: Preoedipal Aspects of Freud's Personality* (Northvale, N.J.: Aronson, 1996), 3. Chapter 1 of this book surveys all of the little that is known of Amalia. Earlier works refer to her as Amalie. Her tombstone, however, reads Amalia, and recent works have used that spelling.

12. Martin Freud, *Sigmund Freud,* 11.

13. Peter Newton, *Freud: From Youthful Dream to Mid-Life Crisis* (New York: Guilford Press, 1995), 37; hereafter cited in text.

14. Ernest Jones, *The Life and Work of Sigmund Freud,* 3 vols. (New York: Basic Books, 1953–1957), 1:9; hereafter cited in text as Jones followed by year of publication, volume, and page numbers.

15. Howard Gardner, *Creating Minds: An Anatomy of Creativity Seen through the Lives of Freud, Einstein, Picasso, Stravinsky, Eliot, Graham, and Gandhi* (New York: Basic Books, 1993), 54.

16. For an excellent concise discussion of Jewish immigration to Vienna and life in the Leopoldstadt, see Hannah S. Decker, *Freud, Dora, and Vienna, 1900* (New York: Free Press, 1991), 16–31; hereafter cited in text.

17. On the uneasy and brief move to constitutional government, see Robert A. Kahn, *A History of the Habsburg Empire, 1826–1915* (Berkeley: University of California Press, 1974), 326–42.

18. The essay is not, in fact, by Goethe. It is now attributed to the Swiss writer Georg Christoph Tobler, who in 1781 spent six months in Weimar and became a friend of Goethe. Interestingly, it does not express the materialist view of nature to which Freud would finally commit himself but a romantic, intuitive, pantheist view associated with the *Naturphilosophie* of earlier in the century. Jones (1953, 1:42–43) argues that Freud, influenced by Goethe, passed through a brief period of enthusiasm for *Naturphilosophie,* which was then replaced by the physical physiology he was taught in medical school. Patrick Mahoney thinks that the vein of *Naturphilosophie* continues as an influence in Freud's life and that his texts bear the stamp of "the physicalist tradition of Humboldtian science, and the intuitive, romantic spirit of *Naturphilosophie.*" See his *Freud as Writer* (New York: International Universities Press, 1982), 162.

19. For more detail on Freud's medical education, see Jones 1953, 1:36–37, and Lucile B. Ritvo, *Darwin's Influence on Freud: A Tale of Two Sciences* (New Haven: Yale University Press, 1990), 113–17; hereafter cited in text.

20. Owen J. Flanagan Jr., *The Science of the Mind* (Cambridge: MIT Press, 1984), 62–63.

21. For a detailed study of Claus, see also Ritvo, 118–49.

22. Vitalism claimed that organic and inorganic matter were different, that biological and physical laws differ, and that biological phenomena cannot be reduced to physical or chemical laws. For vitalists, moreover, living organisms, unlike inert matter, are imbued with a vital or life force and can therefore behave purposefully.

23. From Du Bois-Reymond's letter of 1842, quoted by Robert R. Holt, *Freud Reappraised: A Fresh Look at Psychoanalytic Theory* (New York: Guilford Press, 1989), 149; hereafter cited in text.

24. This is a brief description of a complex subject. For additional detail, see the following: Jones 1953, 1:39–45; David Shakow and David Rapaport, *The Influence of Freud on American Psychology* (Cleveland and New York: Meridian Books, 1968), 33–50; Daniel Yankelovich and William Barrett, *Ego and Instinct: The Psychoanalytic View of Human Nature—Revised* (New York: Random House, 1970), 44–57 (hereafter cited in text); and Peter Amacher, *Freud's Neurological Education and Its Influence on Psychoanalysis* (New York: International Universities Press, 1965). For additional information on Brücke, see Ritvo, 164–69.

25. Erich Fromm, *The Anatomy of Human Destructiveness* (New York: Holt, Rhinehart and Winston, 1973), 472.

26. This is as good a place as any to note that the German Freud uses for drive—*Trieb*—is translated by Strachey in the *Standard Edition* as instinct. Since instincts are usually thought of as automatic reactions typical of a species and drives are supposed to be malleable and responsive to external influences, many were distressed by Strachey's choice. For Strachey's defense of his choice, see *SE,* 1:xxiv–xxvi. In about a half dozen places where Freud uses *Instinkt,* a footnote explains Freud's departure from the more usual *Trieb.* Freud would have been familiar with the debate about the nature of instinct versus drive in human motivation (as in the work of his colleague Sigmund Exner). The *Standard Edition* has come under much criticism in recent years as an adequate and faithful translation of Freud's German. On this issue, see Bruno Bettelheim, *Freud and Man's Soul* (New York: Knopf, 1983) and the essays on translation in Timms and Segal, 177–219.

27. See J. A. C. Brown, *Freud and the Post-Freudians* (Baltimore: Penguin Books, 1964), for a discussion of this division (especially in the work of Karen Horney, Erich Fromm, and Harry Stack Sullivan). See also Ruth Monroe's magisterial *Schools of Psychoanalytic Thought: An Exposition, Critique, and Attempt at Integration* (New York: Henry Holt and Co., 1955).

28. On drive versus relational paradigm, see Stephen A. Mitchell, *Relational Concepts in Psychoanalysis: An Interpretation* (Cambridge, Mass.: Harvard University Press, 1988); hereafter cited in text. Mitchell favors the relational model and sees the shift from drive to relational matrix as a major paradigm shift.

29. See *Letters* for all those published. Most have not yet been published. Jones estimates their number at nine hundred (Jones 1953, 1:99).

30. On the cocaine episode, Jones has an excellent chapter (1953, 1:78–97). See also Robert Byck, ed., *Cocaine Papers by Sigmund Freud* (New York: Stonehill, 1974).

31. On Charcot, see George Frederick Drinka, M.D., *The Birth of Neurosis: Myth, Malady, and the Victorians* (New York: Simon and Schuster, 1984), 74–151; hereafter cited in text. My brief discussion in this whole section is heavily indebted to the two chapters covered by these pages.

32. On hypnosis, Charcot, and Bernheim, see Drinka, 134–51.

33. See, for example, the 1937 essay "Constructions in Analysis" (*SE,* 23:257–69).

34. Ilse Grubrich-Simitis, *Back to Freud's Texts: Making Silent Documents Speak* (New Haven and London: Yale University Press, 1996), 61–62.

Chapter Two

1. Howard Gardner, *Extraordinary Minds: Portraits of Exceptional Individuals and an Examination of Our Extraordinarism* (New York: Basic Books, 1997), 79.

2. On neurasthenia in America and Europe, see Drinka, 184–238.

3. Tom Lutz, *American Nervousness, 1903: An Anecdotal History* (Ithaca and London: Cornell University Press, 1991), 3–7.

4. For example, in the case of Frau Emmy von N. in *Studies on Hysteria,* he uses both massage and hypnosis. He also used electrotherapy for a while after his return from Paris but very quickly understood that it was useless.

5. The drafts are essentially a series of essays either enclosed with Freud's letters to Fliess or else sent separately. Draft A dates from 1892, draft E probably from 1894. See *Freud-Fliess,* 37–38, 39–44, 78–83.

6. I use this essay as a convenient source for my discussion because of its summary nature. Unless otherwise indicated, I am drawing on this essay in describing Freud's classification and theory of the etiology of the neuroses.

7. The term "obsessional neurosis" is original with Freud and is introduced in this paper. Earlier, in "The Neuro-Psychoses of Defence," and in "Obsessions and Phobias" (1895), he refers simply to obsessions. Many recent works on obsession compulsion do not even refer to Freud.

8. In *Five Lectures on Psycho-Analysis* (1910), Freud says that at the time of *Studies on Hysteria* he did not yet hold the view that sexuality was the specific cause of neurosis (*SE,* 11:40).

9. On Breuer, see Albrecht Hirschmüller, *The Life and Work of Josef Breuer: Physiology and Psychoanalysis* (New York: New York University Press, 1989); hereafter cited in text.

10. For the full case, see *SE,* 2:21–47.

11. Henri Ellenberger, "The Story of 'Anna O.': A Critical Review with New Data," *Journal of the History of Behavioral Sciences* 8 (July 1972): 267–79.

12. Mikkel Borch-Jacobsen, *Remembering Anna O: A Century of Mystification* (New York and London: Routledge, 1996), 29–48 (quotation on page 34); hereafter cited in text. This book provides a full account of all the scholarship done on this case.

13. Other critics of the case argue that Anna had an organic illness and that Breuer misdiagnosed her as hysterical. See E. M. Thornton, *The Freudian Fallacy: An Alternate View of Freudian Theory* (Garden City, N.Y.: Dial Press, 1984). Some modern clinicians would see her as having a narcissistic or borderline character disorder, or even as being psychotic. See, for example, Peter Giovacchini, M.D., *A Clinician's Guide to Reading Freud* (New York and London: Aronson, 1982), 41–59, where all these possibilities are entertained.

14. See, for example, *Five Lectures on Psycho-Analysis* (*SE,* 11:9). For the sake of clarification, the hyphenated form of the word "psychoanalysis" is the British spelling, which of course is used by the British Hogarth Press.

15. For brief biographies of these two very interesting women, see Lisa Appignanesi and John Forrester, *Freud's Women* (New York: Basic Books, 1992), 86–103.

16. In the 1890s Freud uses defense and repression interchangeably. After 1900 repression is the word of choice. In 1926, with a revised theory of anxiety as an ego signal rather than dammed-up libido, defense becomes the more general term, of which repression is one kind.

17. On Freud's use of the term "psychical group," see Strachey's discussion in *SE,* 9:100–102.

18. In "The Neuro-Psychoses of Defence" Freud regards phobias as part of the symptomatology of obsession. But in "Obsessions and Phobias: Their Psychic Mechanism and Their Aetiology" (1895), he regards phobia as an anxiety neurosis, hence devoid of psychic content. He has a dilemma. Because anxiety is the predominant emotion in phobia, then phobias must result from a mechanical blocking of libido. Yet as an aspect of obsession a phobia does have psychic content. Even in his 1909 "Analysis of a Phobia in a Five-Year-Old Boy" (better known as the case of Little Hans), he still regards phobias "as syndromes which may form part of various neuroses," and thus "we need not rank them as an independent pathological process" (*SE,* 10:115). For the case of Little Hans he proposes the name "anxiety hysteria" (which did not last). Thus, the meaning of phobia shifts depending on Freud's diagnosis.

19. In both "Heredity and the Aetiology of the Neuroses" and "Further Remarks on the Neuro-Psychoses of Defence," the number of hysterics is given as 13. The discrepancy is unexplained, especially since the three essays were written very close together.

20. Not until "My Views on the Part Played by Sexuality in the Aetiology of the Neuroses" (1906) does Freud publish his changed views on the role of early sexual trauma in causing the neuroses (*SE,* 7:271–79).

21. Jeffrey Moussaieff Masson, *The Assault on Truth: Freud's Suppression of the Seduction Theory* (New York: Penguin Books, 1985).

22. For a recent study that evaluates evidence pro and con regarding the seduction controversy, see Daniel Brown, Alan W. Scheflin, and D. Corydon Hammond, *Memory, Trauma Treatment, and the Law* (New York: Norton, 1998).

23. Paul Robinson, *Freud and His Critics* (Berkeley: University of California Press, 1993), 166. As Robinson notes, Freud's confidence in the seduction theory was always "fragile" (163). See also Gerald N. Izenberg, "Seduced and Abandoned: The Rise and Fall of Freud's Seduction Theory," in Jerome Neu, ed., *The Cambridge Companion to Freud* (Cambridge: Cambridge University Press, 1991), 25–43. Izenberg's discussion is much more detailed than my brief summary.

24. Alexander Grinstein, M.D., *Sigmund Freud's Dreams* (New York: International Universities Press, 1980), 420.

25. For a long and detailed analysis of the *Project,* see Richard Wollheim, *Sigmund Freud* (New York: Viking Press, 1971), 31–58, and Raymond E. Fancher, *Psychoanalytic Psychology: The Development of Freud's Thought* (New York: Norton, 1973), 63–97; both works hereafter cited in text.

26. Harry T. Hunt, *The Multiplicity of Dreams: Memory, Imagination, and Consciousness* (New Haven and London: Yale University Press, 1989), 15.

27. For an exhaustive study of all of Freud's dreams in *The Interpretation of Dreams,* see Grinstein, *Sigmund Freud's Dreams.* On the self-analysis, see Didier Anzieu, *Freud's Self-Analysis,* trans. Peter Graham (Madison, Conn.: International Universities Press, 1986) and Mark Kanzer, M.D. and Jules Glenn, M.D., eds., *Freud and His Self-Analysis* (New York: Aronson, 1983).

28. Material on Fliess is available in all Freud biographies (see bibliography). For a detailed intellectual analysis of his work, see Frank J. Sulloway, *Freud, Biologist of the Mind: Beyond the Psychoanalytic Legend* (New York: Basic Books, 1974), 135–70.

29. For the letter in which Freud described the scene to Fliess, see *Freud-Fliess,* 116–18.

Chapter Three

1. Leonard Shengold, M.D., "The Metaphor of the Journey in *The Interpretation of Dreams,*" in Kanzer and Glenn, eds., *Freud and His Self-Analysis,* 51–65; Stanley Edgar Hyman, *The Tangled Bank: Darwin, Marx, Frazer, and Freud as Imaginative Writers* (New York: Atheneum, 1962), 332–38 (quotation on 336).

2. Charles Rycroft, *The Innocence of Dreams* (London: Hogarth Press, 1979), 77–78.

3. Freud is not always sure that secondary revision is part of the dream work. In "An Evidential Dream" (1913) he seems to exclude it (*SE,* 12:275).

4. From the perspective of psychoanalysis, the word "subconscious" is meaningless, since it fails to distinguish between unconscious and preconscious.

5. Freud uses the word "system" in *The Interpretation of Dreams* (*SE,* 5:614–15) and thus prepares the way for his definition of the systematic, as opposed to the topographical and dynamic, unconscious in "The Unconscious" (1915). With this concept he attempts to look at the unconscious in terms of its mode of operation rather than from the point of view of consciousness (as do the topographical and dynamic views).

6. Cathexis is Strachey's word for Freud's *Besetzung* (occupation). Cathexis means a quantity of psychic energy attached to a person, an idea, or an image. To cathect means to invest with psychic energy.

I need also to clarify the word "idea." Technically, after 1900 repression is directed against an instinctual impulse instead of the memory of a traumatic event, as in Freud's earlier clinical view. But instinctual impulses are known only by their psychic representations such as wishes, fantasies, and memories. These are what he means by ideas—the psychic representation of an instinct—not, say, philosophical or scientific ideas. The confusion (to me, at least) probably comes from Strachey's translation of Freud's *Vorstellung* (which means idea but also picture, image, or representation) only as idea.

7. Unpleasure principle is precisely the right term, though Freud sometimes refers to the "unpleasure-pleasure principle." In 1911 ("Formulation on the Two Principles of Mental Functioning") he uses simply "pleasure principle" for the first time, and most commentators have adopted this change. But it is not accurate. In 1924 ("The Economic Problem of Masochism") he does finally try to distinguish between positive and negative pleasure. But until then the pleasure principle always means a discharge, not an accumulation, of excitation.

8. Fiction because, as he admits in "Formulations on the Two Principles of Mental Functioning," an "organization which was a slave to the pleasure principle and neglected the reality of the external world could not maintain itself alive for the shortest time, so that it could not have come into existence at all" (*SE,* 12:220 n). Freud has often been criticized for this evolutionarily impossible scenario.

9. Jonathan Lear is puzzled that Freud fails to notice the implication of the fact that the hallucinated satisfaction is based on a prior real satisfaction at a real breast. Where Freud sees the secondary process developing from the primary process, Lear suggests just the opposite. See *Love and Its Place in Nature: A Philosophical Interpretation of Freudian Psychoanalysis* (New York: Farrar, Straus, and Giroux, 1990), 75–87; hereafter cited in text.

10. In "Remarks on the Theory and Practice of Dream-Interpretation" (1923), Freud refers to dreams from above and dreams from below (*SE,* 19:111).

11. As he says in "An Evidential Dream," "one cannot put the wish-fulfilling character of dreams on a par with their character as warnings, admissions, attempts at solution, etc., without denying the concept of a psychical

dimension of depth—that is to say, without denying the standpoint of psychoanalysis" (*SE,* 12:275). The fact that Freud doesn't always discuss repressed infantile wishes in his analysis of dreams should not lead to the conclusion that they are not for him the primary motivational factor in the construction of dreams. Freud admits only one exception to the wish fulfillment theory—that of traumatic dreams that repeat the traumatic situation, as in shell-shocked veterans of World War I (*SE,* 22:28). He insists that anxiety dreams represent failures of the censor and that punishment dreams represent a wish for punishment. He does, indeed, push the wish fulfillment theory to its limits.

12. Richard M. Jones, *The New Psychology of Dreaming* (New York: Viking Press, 1970), 67–109; hereafter cited in text.

13. All mammals and some birds have REM periods, which are now understood as a phylogenetically very ancient physiological state.

14. J. Allan Hobson, *The Dreaming Brain* (New York: Basic Books, 1988), 203–22; hereafter cited in text.

15. Wilma Bucci, *Psychoanalysis and Cognitive Science: A Multiple Code Theory* (New York: Guilford Press, 1997), 249; hereafter cited in text.

16. Paul Kline, *Psychology and Freudian Theory: An Introduction* (London and New York: Methuen, 1984), 95; hereafter cited in text.

17. For Jung's view see C. G. Jung, *Dreams,* trans. R. F. C. Hull (Princeton: Princeton University Press, 1974), 23–83.

18. The intrinsic symbolic nature of the dream is an important issue, as Freud himself recognizes. As he says in the analysis of one of his own dreams (the botanical monograph) in which he came upon a memory of his father giving him an illustrated book to destroy, "It may perhaps be doubted whether this memory really had any share in determining the form taken by the content of the dream or whether it was not rather that the process of analysis built up the connection subsequently" (*SE,* 4:191). That is, association to the dream may lead to a given scene, but that does not prove that this scene is the cause of the dream or that it is a factor in the dream work. Associations to meaningful life problems could as easily come from nonsymbolic (meaningless) as from symbolic dream elements.

19. Ernest Jones actually suggested the term "parapraxis" in a 1911 paper entitled "The Psychopathology of Everyday Life," in *Papers on Psycho-Analysis* (Boston: Beacon Press, 1961), 24–86.

20. Adolph Grünbaum, *The Foundations of Psychoanalysis: A Philosophical Critique* (Berkeley: University of California Press, 1984), 190–215.

21. Donald Levy, *Freud among the Philosophers: The Psychoanalytic Unconscious and Its Philosophical Critics* (New Haven and London: Yale University Press, 1996), 159–65; quotations on 160, 161.

22. Sebastiano Timpanaro, *The Freudian Slip: Psychoanalysis and Textual Criticism,* trans. Kate Soper (Atlantic Highland, N.J.: Humanities Press, 1976).

23. E. H. Gombrich, "Freud's Aesthetics," *Encounter* 26 (January 1966): 30–40; Norman O. Brown, *Life against Death: The Psychoanalytical*

Meaning of History (Middletown, Conn.: Wesleyan University Press, 1959), 55–67; hereafter cited in text. In a view of art based on an analogy with jokes, the artist is clearly oriented both toward reality and the unconscious but never overwhelmed by either. Assuming the correctness of substituting art for jokes, this is a more positive view of art and artist than Freud often takes. Very often he portrays the artist as fleeing reality for the substitute gratification (that is, the fantasy world) of art. See the 1908 essay "Creative Writers and Day-Dreaming" (*SE,* 9:143–53) and the conclusion of Lecture 23 in *Introductory Lectures on Psycho-Analysis* (*SE,* 16:375–77).

24. See also Gay's essay "Reading Freud through Freud's Reading," in *Reading Freud: Explorations and Entertainments* (New Haven and London: Yale University Press, 1990), 95–124. For additional material on Freud and jokes, see Elliott Orin, *The Jokes of Sigmund Freud: A Study in Human and Jewish Identity* (Philadelphia: University of Pennsylvania Press, 1984).

25. I have previously discussed Freud's uses of the word *Trieb* (drive) and its meaning as opposed to *Instinkt.* Because of Strachey's translation, I will use instinct even where I mean drive.

26. Morris N. Eagle, *Recent Developments in Psychoanalysis: A Critical Evaluation* (New York: McGraw-Hill, 1984), 118, 15; hereafter cited in text.

27. See, for example, Jay R. Greenberg and Stephen A. Mitchell, *Object Relations in Psychoanalytic Theory* (Cambridge: Harvard University Press, 1983); hereafter cited in text. This book surveys the many contemporary psychoanalytic responses to this issue. But see also Malcolm Owen Slavin and Daniel Kriegman, *The Adaptive Design of the Human Psyche: Psychoanalysis, Evolutionary Biology, and the Therapeutic Process* (New York: Guilford Press, 1992) (hereafter cited in text) for a spirited defense of drive theory in evolutionary terms. Endogenous drives, the authors say, are "quite likely to have evolved as a safeguard for self-interest" (164). For Slavin and Kriegman (and many others) the issue is not between drive theory and no drive theory but between drive defined in terms of the tension reduction model and drive defined as internal motivating systems or programs that regulate responses rather than discharging accumulating energy. In terms of contemporary evolutionary psychology and neuroscience, such programs are by no means scientifically untenable.

In my presentation of Freud's pervasive use of a drive reduction model in his theory of sexuality and the neuroses and in his revised theory of the instincts in 1920, I take the problems with his position as given and as a serious issue for modern psychoanalysis.

28. Jonathan Miller, *States of Mind* (New York: Pantheon Books, 1987), 237.

29. In "The Infantile Genital Organization: An Interpolation into the Theory of Sexuality" (1923), Freud modifies his belief that full genital primacy must await puberty and also inserts a phallic stage between the anal sadistic and the genital in which only the male genital is known by the child (*SE,* 19:141–45). Though the pregenital stages were only added to *Three Essays* in

1915, Freud had earlier introduced the concept in 1913 in "The Disposition to Obsessional Neurosis" (*SE,* 12:317–26).

30. See "On the Sexual Theories of Children" (*SE,* 9:209–26).

31. For an example of sublimation and both artistic and scientific creativity in one person, see "Leonardo da Vinci and a Memory of His Childhood" (1910); on reaction formation and character see "Character and Anal Erotism" (1908).

32. On the evidence for Eagle's statement, see 10–16.

33. For a detailed discussion and analysis of these responses, see Eagle, *Recent Developments in Psychoanalysis* and Mitchell, *Relational Concepts in Psychoanalysis.*

34. As described in the 1915 essay "The Unconscious" (*SE,* 14:187). I am aware that "Repression" and "The Unconscious" do not come within the period I am covering in this chapter. Both essays, however, represent attempts to consolidate ideas with which Freud is operating during this period.

35. But Freud's description of the three stages of repression in his 1911 "Psycho-Analytic Notes on an Autobiographical Account of a Case of Paranoia (Dementia Paranoides)"—better known as the Schreber case—does not support my conclusion. Here, it seems, the ego only affects repression proper (*SE,* 12:67–68). Maybe, as Wollheim suggests, the explanation for primal repression is quasi-biological—that is, based on Freud's postulation of organic repression that derives "from man's adoption of the upright posture" and his consequent devaluation of the olfactory stimuli associated with the anal and genital zones (Wollheim, 160). Biologically programmed, organic repression would thus be the result of evolving from hominid to human. The possibility that many humans will be neurotic is born at the same time. For such ideas in Freud, see *Freud-Fliess,* 223, 279–81; *SE,* 7:177–78; *SE,* 21:99–100 n.

Freud not only denies that psychoanalysis is pansexual, he also refuses to be an advocate of complete sexual liberation as the way to human happiness. He certainly advocates a less repressive attitude toward genital sexuality, but he never for a moment thinks that it is possible either to liberate or satisfy the infantile component instincts. In short, Freud is no Wilhelm Reich who preaches the power of the orgasm to free humankind. On the other hand, Freud's naturalizing of polymorphous perversity does constitute a revolutionary challenge to the view that adult genital sexuality for the purpose of procreation is the only natural sexuality.

36. Actually this is backwards. Chronologically, as his letters to Fliess show, Freud discovered the compromise formation of symptoms and then applied that formula to dreams (*Freud-Fliess,* 189, 217, 239, 380). As Freud says, dream interpretation began and continued as a therapeutic tool when his free-associating patients told him, among other things, their dreams (*SE,* 4:100–101).

37. I return to this case in the next chapter.

38. In "From the History of an Infantile Neurosis" (1918), Freud analyzes another childhood phobia—that of the Wolf Man (because of his dream of the white wolves), whose real name was Sergei Pankejeff, a young Russian aristocrat who is surely the most famous psychoanalytic patient of the century (*SE,* 17:7–133). The Wolf Man's phobia, however, differs in many ways from that of Little Hans—not least in being the precursor of an obsessional neurosis. For Freud's comparison of the two cases, see *SE,* 20:101–10. Hans, incidentally, was Herbert Graf, son of Viennese music historian Max Graf. For many years Herbert was stage director of the Metropolitan Opera in New York.

39. This is only a sketch of a very complex case history, which should be read in full. Ambivalence, incidentally, is a word often associated with Freud and psychoanalysis but was actually coined by Eugen Bleuler (1857–1939), director of the Burghölzli Mental Hospital near Zurich and Jung's immediate supervisor. He was ambivalent in his enthusiasm for psychoanalysis, to Freud's annoyance.

40. His father had opposed his relationship with the lady, just as he had opposed his four- or five-year-old son's erotic interest in his governess and other girls.

41. Freud uses the word "complex" as early as the *Project* and *Studies on Hysteria* in a way that is compatible with its use in the phrase "nuclear complex." But it is likely that its appearance in the Rat Man case and thereafter was influenced by Jung's use of the term to describe results obtained by him in word-association tests he conducted in Zurich beginning around 1902. According to Jungian analyst Anthony Stevens in *Archetypes: A Natural History of the Self* (New York: Quill, 1983), a complex is a "group of interconnected ideas and feelings which exert a dynamic effect on conscious experience and on behaviour" (297).

42. This is, of course, from the boy's point of view. Until he turns to the study of feminine development in the 1920s, Freud tends to assume that for the girl the situation is simply a mirror image of the boy's.

43. My discussion of the Oedipus complex here is indebted to the excellent paper by Bennett Simon and Rachel B. Blass, "The Development and Vicissitudes of Freud's Ideas on the Oedipus Complex," in Neu, ed., *The Cambridge Companion to Freud,* 161–74; hereafter cited in text.

44. The meaning of an incestuous object choice in the Oedipus complex needs to be clarified. People still ridicule the idea of the Oedipus complex as asserting that a boy wants to sleep with his mother. That is not what Freud means, as he makes very clear in a passage from *The Question of Lay Analysis* (1926). It is true, he says here, that the child's wishes toward the parent of the opposite sex are not just for affection but for sensual satisfaction—"so far, that is, as the child's powers of imagination allow." But the child "never guesses the actual facts of sexual intercourse" and as a rule these wishes (even for boys) "culminate in the intention to bear, or in some indefinable way, to procreate a

baby" (*SE,* 20:213). Freud does refer to this first choice of object as incestuous, but without the implication of adult genital sexuality. This is very different from the parody extant in popular culture and among many academics.

45. For a study of the failure to combine affection and sensuality in loving one person, see "On the Universal Tendency to Debasement in the Sphere of Love" (*SE,* 11:179–90). This is one of three essays by Freud on the psychology of love. The other two are "A Special Type of Object Choice Made by Man" (1910) and "The Taboo of Virginity" (1918).

46. In recent years Westermarck has achieved some vindication of his thesis for some people. The case for Westermarck rests on two case studies—one of the Taiwanese and Chinese form of marriage in which young girls are adopted by parents with young sons, the other of young people in Israel's kibbutzim. From these studies it was concluded that human beings tend to lack sexual interest in people with whom they have had prolonged prepubescent contact. Combined with ethological studies of incest avoidance among close relatives of various species in the wild, these studies have convinced many researchers that humans are genetically programmed to avoid incest. See on this fascinating subject, Carl N. Degler, *In Search of Human Nature: The Decline and Revival of Darwinism in American Social Thought* (New York: Oxford University Press, 1991), 245–69. But see also Marvin Harris's skeptical evaluation of this material (except that he omits the ethological data) in *Our Kind* (New York: Harper and Row, 1989), 198–201. Harris notes historical cases of brother-sister incest as well as the prevalence of sexual abuse of children (especially father-daughter incest) in the United States today. Allen W. Johnson and Douglass Price-Williams question the Westermarck hypothesis on two grounds. First, they note that brother-sister incest (usually among siblings raised together) "appears to be rather common," far more common than father-daughter incest or the very rare mother-son incest. Second, if siblings "have no interest in marrying each other, then why prohibit it?" This second point is, of course, also made by Freud and Frazer. See *Oedipus Ubiquitous: The Family Complex in World Folk Literature* (Stanford: Stanford University Press, 1996), 28. I think this issue is far from settled.

47. I know of one exception (though by a sociologist, not an anthropologist): C. R. Badcock, *The Psychoanalysis of Culture* (Oxford: Basil Blackwell, 1980). Maybe there are others. This is, by the way, a very interesting book.

48. Edwin R. Wallace, IV, *Freud and Anthropology: A History and Reappraisal* (New York: International Universities Press, 1983), 179–80. My brief synopsis here is a very inadequate summary of a complex intellectual shift from nineteenth- to twentieth-century anthropology. A careful reading of Wallace's book is essential for an understanding of the issues involved.

49. Robert A. Paul, *Moses and Civilization: The Meaning Behind Freud's Myth* (New Haven and London: Yale University Press, 1996), 3–4 (Paul's italics).

50. Paul Roazen, *Freud: Political and Social Thought* (New York: Knopf, 1968), 153–58.

51. Colin Tudge, *The Time before History: 5 Million Years of Human Impact* (New York: Scribner's, 1996), 108; hereafter cited in text.

52. No one seems to notice Freud's implicit repudiation of one of Lamarck's other laws of evolution when, in *Beyond the Pleasure Principle* (1920), he rejects the idea of an "instinct towards perfection" at work in human beings (*SE,* 18:42). In other words, like Darwin, Freud sees no evidence of purpose (teleology) in evolution.

53. Sigmund Freud, *A Phylogenetic Fantasy: Overview of the Transference Neuroses,* edited and with an essay by Ilse Grubrich-Simitis, translated by Axel Hoffer and Peter T. Hoffer (Cambridge: Belknap Press of Harvard University Press, 1987), 13. In this essay the primal father does not just drive the sons of the primal horde away. He castrates them.

54. On Freud and Haeckel, see Ritvo, 74–98. Wallace notes in *Freud and Anthropology* that many of the evolutionary anthropologists Freud read as a young man and in preparing for *Totem and Taboo* subscribed to the biogenetic law. For a contemporary critique of this law see Stephen Jay Gould, *Ontogeny and Phylogeny* (Cambridge: Belknap Press of Harvard University Press, 1977). For a cautious and tentative contemporary use of this law in a study of the evolution of the human mind, see Steven Mithen, *The Prehistory of the Mind: The Cognitive Origins of Art, Religion, and Science* (London: Thames and Hudson, 1996), 61–72. Maybe this idea isn't as dead as some of Freud's critics claim.

55. On this subject see the fascinating discussion by Johnson and Price-Williams in *Oedipus Ubiquitous* on the evolutionary basis of the Oedipus complex (93–96). They admit, however, that "we still do not have a language for talking about the possibility that the Oedipus complex and the oedipal tale have some kind of structural analogue or complement in the human genome" (94).

Chapter Four

1. On the meetings see Herman Nunberg and Ernst Federn, *Minutes of the Vienna Psychoanalytic Society,* 3 vols. (New York: International Universities Press, 1962, 1967, 1974).

2. Ernest Jones was in the audience and, after the congress, traveled to Vienna to visit Freud.

3. For a detailed account of these events, see Gay 1988, 197–243. On Jung, see Linda Donn, *Freud and Jung: Years of Friendship, Years of Loss* (New York: Scribner's, 1988). One of the best readings of the inner drama of the Freud-Jung friendship is Peter Homans, *Jung in Context: Modernity and the Making of a Psychology* (Chicago and London: University of Chicago Press, 1979), 42–73.

4. For an account of this Committee by the man who suggested it, see Jones 1955, 2:152–67.

5. Much of what he says in these essays is beautifully summarized in *Introductory Lectures on Psycho-Analysis* (Lectures 27 and 28) and in *The Question of Lay Analysis* (1926). Lay analysis means the practice of psychoanalysis by someone other than a physician. Freud favored lay analysis because he thought that psychoanalysis had applications in fields far beyond medicine and because a psychoanalyst did not really need a medical background to treat neurosis.

6. Even so, psychoanalysts have always debated, and continue to do so, various aspects of Freud's recommendations and how and when to use them. In fact, contemporary analysts by no means follow all of these recommendations. For a detailed study of continuities with, variations on, and debates about Freud's ideas on technique, see Steven J. Ellman, *Freud's Technique Papers: A Contemporary Perspective* (Northvale, N.J.: Aronson, 1991); hereafter cited in text.

7. Freud made notes only in the evenings, never during sessions. He wanted nothing to interfere with his evenly suspended attention.

8. There is no doubt that Freud is correct in seeing himself as deaf to the transference. But this is not his only mistake. Like a surgeon with a new operation, he is far too ready to apply to Dora his new ideas on sexuality at the expense of recognizing the reality of her personal situation, as when he says of Dora's feeling of disgust when she was 14 and Herr K. kissed her on the lips: "I should without question consider a person hysterical in whom an occasion for sexual excitement elicited feelings that were preponderantly or exclusively unpleasurable" (*SE,* 7:28). As Gay says, the "rage to cure was upon him." "What is astonishing about the case history of Dora," he continues, "is not that Freud delayed it for four years, but that he published it at all" (Gay 1988, 20).

Dora remains a controversial case. See, for example, the following works for critical responses to it: Charles Bernheimer and Claire Kahane, eds., *In Dora's Case: Freud—Hysteria—Feminism* (New York: Columbia University Press, 1985); Hannah Decker, *Freud, Dora, and Vienna, 1900;* and Patrick J. Mahoney, *Freud's Dora: A Psychoanalytic, Historical, and Textual Study* (New Haven and London: Yale University Press, 1996).

Dora was Ida Bauer, whose brother Otto was one of the leading Austro-Marxists of the 1920s and 1930s. See Peter Loewenburg, "Austro-Marxism and Revolution: Otto Bauer, Freud's 'Dora' Case, and the Crisis of the First Austrian Republic," in *Decoding the Past: The Psychohistorical Approach* (New York: Knopf, 1983), 161–204.

9. In *Introductory Lectures on Psycho-Analysis,* Freud explains resistance from the positive transference somewhat differently: positive transference leads to resistance "if as an affectionate trend it has become so powerful, and betrays signs of its origin in a sexual need so clearly, that it inevitably provokes an internal opposition to itself" (*SE,* 16:443).

10. Countertransference has become very important in contemporary psychoanalysis in a way it never was for Freud. He uses the term only four

times. Its many dangers are certainly among the reasons for his recommendation of a training analysis for all aspiring psychoanalysts. I doubt that he would approve of the current emphasis on the role of countertransference feelings as a clue to the patient's unconscious communications.

There is a considerable literature on whether and how well Freud followed his own recommendations on technique. This is a running theme in Ellman's *Freud's Technique Papers* (286–311). For a variety of views on Freud's behavior—sometimes approving, sometimes not—see Mark Kanzer, M.D. and Jules Glenn, M.D., eds., *Freud and His Patients* (Northvale, N.J.: Aronson, 1993). For an account of interviews with 10 of Freud's former patients, see Paul Roazen, *How Freud Worked: First-Hand Accounts of Patients* (Northvale, N.J.: Aronson, 1995). For recent analyses of two of Freud's case histories, see Patrick J. Mahoney, *Cries of the Wolf Man* (New York: International Universities Press, 1984) and *Freud and the Rat Man* (New Haven and London: Yale University Press, 1986). For additional material on the Wolf Man, see *The Wolf-Man by the Wolf-Man,* ed. Muriel Gardner (New York: Basic Books, 1971). This book contains the Wolf Man's own memories, Freud's case, an account of his later analysis with Ruth Mack Brunswick, and portraits of the Wolf Man in later life by Muriel Gardner.

11. All psychotherapies are equally hard to evaluate and for the same reasons. For a more detailed survey of the literature on scientific appraisals of Freud's theories, see Paul Kline, *Fact and Fantasy in Freudian Theory* (London: Methuen, 1981). For a very negative view on the evidence for the therapeutic efficacy of psychoanalysis, see Malcolm MacMillan, *The Completed Arc: Freud Evaluated* (Cambridge: MIT Press, 1997), 563–89. For a more balanced but equally critical analysis, see Stephen Frosh, *For and Against Psychoanalysis* (London and New York: Routledge, 1997), 77–146; hereafter cited in text. For a comprehensive study of problems in all psychotherapies (including psychoanalysis), see Robert T. Fancher, *Culture of Healing: Correcting the Image of American Mental Health Care* (New York: Freeman, 1995).

12. Quoted in both German and English in Shakow and Rapaport, 129 n.

13. This doesn't mean that everything Grünbaum says is true, including his famous claim that Freud's tally argument—that is, that only interpretations that tally with what is real in the patient will be therapeutically efficacious—is the sole basis for all of his therapeutic and theoretical claims. For interesting replies to Grünbaum on this and other points, see Levy, 132–44; Robinson, 209–31; and David Sachs, "In Fairness to Freud: A Critical Notice of *The Foundations of Psychoanalysis,* by Adolf Grünbaum," in Neu, ed., *The Cambridge Companion to Freud,* 309–38.

14. Donald P. Spence, *Narrative Truth and Historical Truth: Meaning and Interpretation in Psychoanalysis* (New York: Norton, 1982), 230; Spence's italics. Spence is generally thought of as an advocate of hermeneutic psychoanalysis—that is, a psychoanalysis whose true focus is the human world of interpreted meaning rather than a natural science studying cause and effect. Its aim is to

bring psychoanalysis back to Freud's original observations on the conscious and unconscious meanings and intentions of dreams, parapraxes, and neurotic symptoms and to abandon the natural science of drive theory. In Freud, of course, these two domains interact. See also Spence's *The Freudian Metaphor: Toward Paradigm Change in Psychoanalysis* (New York: Norton, 1987); hereafter cited in text. For the book that probably started this tradition of psychoanalytic thinking, see Paul Ricoeur, *Freud and Philosophy: An Essay in Interpretation,* trans. Denis Savage (New Haven and London: Yale University Press, 1970). Like everything else in psychoanalysis, hermeneutic psychoanalysis has both supporters and critics. For a trenchant negative critique of hermeneutic psychoanalysis, see Eagle, 164–71.

15. Freud's view that homosexuality, like heterosexuality, develops is consistent with his view that there is no sexual essence at birth.

16. Dementia praecox was coined by Emil Kraepelin (1856–1926)—the nosologist of the psychoses—in 1893. Bleuler later coined the word "schizophrenia" in 1908, and this term gradually replaced Kraepelin's. Freud never abandoned his belief that psychoses (he calls them narcissistic disorders) were not amenable to psychoanalytic therapy because of the incapacity of psychotics to develop transferences. But he was wrong. Psychotics do develop transferences, but it takes time and patience on the part of the therapist.

17. For many analysts, the idea of primary narcissism before object relations makes no sense. See, for example, Michael Balint, *The Basic Fault: Therapeutic Aspects of Regression* (London and New York: Tavistock, 1979), 46–51. Infant research suggests that Freud may be confusing a normal, early cognitive stage of development with adult pathology.

18. As Robert Holt has shown, metapsychology can be a very hard term to define (15–33). Freud gives a simple definition in "The Unconscious": "I propose that when we have succeeded in describing a psychical process in its dynamic, topographical and economic aspects, we should speak of it as a *metapsychological* presentation" (*SE,* 14:181; Freud's italics). I have already defined topographical and dynamic. Economic refers to the distribution of quantities of energy and thus to the tension reduction principle. As Grubrich-Simitis observes, however, not all works in which Freud describes psychical processes in these three ways are metapsychology. "It is customary today," she says, "to count as Freud's major metapsychological works only those writings in which he unfolds his theoretical thoughts explicitly, exclusively, and in detail at the highest level of abstraction" (Grubrich-Simitis 1987, 85).

19. And why such a repudiation? Because such stimuli produce unpleasurable accumulations of energy that must be discharged. Contemporary infant researchers do not see a primal hatred of objects; they see stimulus seeking as an inborn cognitive and affective response to the world.

20. I have entitled this section "Eros and Thanatos," although Freud never used the word "Thanatos," which was introduced by Paul Federn, except in conversation (Jones 1957, 3:273). Yet many writers refer casually to Freud's

concept of Thanatos as if it were a term he used. This is a harmless but careless practice.

21. For additional material on Spielrein, see Alexander Etkind, *Eros of the Impossible: The History of Psychoanalysis in Russia,* trans. Noah and Maria Rubins (New York: Westview Press, 1997), 132–78.

22. Even the sexual instincts are conservative, though they appear to perpetuate rather than end life. They are conservative in bringing back earlier states of living organisms (the gene cell reproduces the beginning of development), in being resistant to external influence, and in preserving life. Freud strains very hard to make even the opponent of the death instinct just as conservative as its opposite.

23. One of the childhood games he describes is that of his grandson who played at staging the disappearance and return of his mother by repeatedly throwing a reel over the edge of his cot and then pulling it back, at the same time saying *fort* (gone) and *da* (there). I doubt that Freud thinks his grandson's play was demonic, though it was repetitious. It's not fully clear that Freud sees play as beyond the pleasure principle.

24. Max Schur, M.D., *Freud: Living and Dying* (New York: International Universities Press, 1972), 320–28. For another critique of the repetition compulsion, see Paul F. Stepansky, *A History of Aggression in Freud* (New York: International Universities Press, 1977), 10–13. The idea of a compulsion to repeat first appears in "The 'Uncanny' " (1919).

25. Stepansky views Freud's theory of life and death instincts as nonempirical and vitalist (Stepansky, 8). Lear, on the other hand, views Freud's expansion of libido into Eros as an important discovery about the nature of love (Lear, 147–55).

26. In *Beyond the Pleasure Principle* Freud says only that there might be primary masochism. In "The Economic Problem of Masochism" (1924), he takes primary masochism as a certainty (*SE,* 19:159–70). The importance of sadism as evidence for the death instinct is emphasized in a statement in *An Outline of Psycho-Analysis*: the death instinct "remains silent" so long as it operates internally; "it only comes to our notice when it is diverted outwards as an instinct of destruction" (*SE,* 23:150).

27. Herbert Marcuse, *Eros and Civilization: A Philosophical Inquiry into Freud* (New York: Vintage Books, 1962); Norman O. Brown, *Life against Death.*

28. For a good but brief overview of some contemporary views, see "Theories of Aggression" in Peter Gay, *The Cultivation of Hatred: The Bourgeois Experience, Victoria to Freud* (New York: Norton, 1993), 529–36. For a comprehensive analysis of aggression, see Fromm, *The Anatomy of Human Destructiveness.* I was surprised to come across the following statement in Sherwin B. Nuland's *The Wisdom of the Body* (New York: Knopf, 1997): "the human brain has . . . engaged itself in the instinctual battle between stability and chaos, echoing up from its deepest cellular self. That battle is expressed in the psychological conflict between Eros and Thanatos—the forces of love (and therefore life) against

the forces of the death instinct" (362). He doesn't cite Freud, but this statement is exactly what Freud means—a battle built into the very structure of the basic units of life. Nuland, incidentally, is a surgeon, not a psychoanalyst.

29. Among the reducible concepts of the social bond, Freud includes the herd instinct proposed by Wilfred Trotter in *Instincts of the Herd in War and Peace* (1916).

30. Paul Roazen argues that the top-and-bottom analysis that Freud uses (that is, leaders and led, with nothing in between) is the traditional liberal, Enlightenment view of the state and the individual with no group in between. In order, he says, "to sweep away the chaos of feudal restrictions," liberals had to rely on the "sharp instrument" of enlightened despotism. Freud thus fails to see or analyze the "vast range of social institutions that cushion the relationship of the individual to his leader." See *Freud: Political and Social Thought,* 231.

31. Thomas Mann, a friend and admirer of Freud's, captures the hypnotic aspect of group formation as a form of being in love in his allegory on the rise of Italian fascism, *Mario and the Magician* (1929). I don't think Freud was prophetic, but his portrait of the leader as hypnotist is certainly an interesting anticipation of Hitler.

Chapter Five

1. For a sampling of the regular and careful notes kept by Freud's Viennese surgeon over a 16-year period, see Jones 1957, 3:468–95. For an account of Freud's cancer from 1923 to his death, see Schur, 347–529.

2. In terms of historical influence, it is certainly the origin of ego psychology (which became so important in the United States) and led directly to the founding works of that tradition: Anna Freud's *The Ego and the Mechanisms of Defense* (1936) and Heinz Hartmann's *Ego Psychology and the Problem of Adaptation* (1939).

3. Strachey's note at this point in "The Unconscious" refers to a footnote added in 1920 to *Three Essays* in which Freud discusses pubertal fantasies, including the primal fantasies of seduction, castration, and overhearing the parents in sexual intercourse; womb fantasies; and the Oedipus complex (I assume he means Oedipal fantasies).

4. The tension reduction principle thus continues into the structural model.

5. As late as the writing of *An Outline of Psycho-Analysis* (published posthumously in 1940), Freud stood by his view that the ego develops from the id (*SE,* 23:145). Many later ego psychologists—notably Heinz Hartmann—do not accept this view. Hartmann sees an adaptive albeit undeveloped ego structure as present from birth (48–56). This view would certainly appear to be confirmed by infant research.

6. Freud's idea of consciousness originating in perception of stimuli is similar to (though far less developed than) Nicholas Humphrey's position in *A*

History of the Mind: Evolution and the Birth of Consciousness (New York: Simon and Schuster, 1992).

7. Bucci argues—and cites other analysts in support of her position—that the structural model does not resolve ambiguities about the status of organized fantasies, dreams, and other primary process events. The problem is that, since Freud continues to view primary and secondary process as two qualitatively different entities, it is hard to see how condensation and displacement (as primary process mechanisms) can be used by the secondary process. The answer may be that sometimes he views them as primary process mechanisms and sometimes as defensive mechanisms (as in the dream work). But this solution still leaves an ambiguity (Bucci, 27). Perhaps Lear is right that "Freud should not have so segregated primary from secondary process" (Lear, 181). Lear correctly sees that Freud's segregation of the two is the result of his energy discharge theory.

8. In this passage Freud clearly attributes repression to the ego ideal. Yet in "The Dissolution of the Oedipus Complex" (1924), he writes of the ego's "turning away from the Oedipus complex" as repression and adds that later repressions come about with the aid of the superego, which is only being formed at the end of the Oedipus complex (*SE,* 19:177). In *New Introductory Lectures on Psycho-Analysis,* he sees repression as the work of the superego carried out either by itself or "by the ego in obedience to its orders" (*SE,* 22:69). Presumably repression prior to the dissolution of the Oedipus complex is effected by the ego. The formation of the superego, then, "provides the line of demarcation" between primal repression and repression proper (*SE,* 20:94).

9. I have earlier referred to Freud's insertion of a phallic phase between the anal sadistic and the genital stages of libidinal development in "The Infantile Genital Organization" (1923). Though Freud had long been aware of castration as an element in the neuroses (Little Hans and the Rat Man), he was not ready until this essay to bring forward the castration complex as a central motive in the dissolution of the Oedipus complex. In earlier accounts the affectionate feelings for the father are the main force of repression.

10. But see Hans Loewald's essay "The Waning of the Oedipus Complex" in *Papers on Psychoanalysis* (New Haven and London: Yale University Press, 1980), 384–404. Loewald contends that, no matter how repressed or destroyed, the Oedipus complex reappears in adolescence and later in both normal people and neurotics.

11. Melanie Klein, "The Early Development of Conscience in the Child," in *Love, Guilt, and Reparation and Other Works, 1921–1945* (London: Hogarth Press, 1981).

12. From this idea comes Freud's analysis of aggression and guilt in *Civilization and Its Discontents.* For Freud's discussion of the fusion and defusion of the two instincts, see 41–42. It is worth emphasizing that the idea of fusing and defusing instincts and Freud's use of it to explain the regressive turning of destructiveness against the ego is entirely speculative. In spite of Freud's inter-

changeable use of superego and ego ideal in *The Ego and the Id,* his emphasis on the superego as a pure culture of the death instinct directed at the ego is very different from the ego ideal as an imagined perfection. For his attempt to maintain the concept of the ego ideal as an aspect of the superego, see *SE,* 22:58–65.

13. See, for example, his discussion in *Inhibitions, Symptoms, and Anxiety,* where he argues that the decisive factor in the ego's ability to repress the id lies in its being an organization, unlike the id (*SE,* 20:97).

14. As a clinician who rejects the seething-cauldron-of-chaos metaphor for the id, Eagle proposes that this famous formula means two things: that what is "impersonal and disowned comes to be owned and experienced as part of oneself"; and that a person must find in his or her "personal aims and desires" a place for "aspects of our vital biological nature and needs" (203, 207). This position, or something very like it, is held by many modern therapists who do not share what they see as Freud's belief in an innate antagonism between our biological nature and the ego.

15. Freud's belief in bisexuality goes back to his friendship with Fliess, who interested him in the idea. In a letter of 1 August 1899, he says, "But bisexuality! You are certainly right about it. I am accustoming myself to regarding every sexual act as a process in which four individuals are involved" (*Freud-Fliess,* 364).

16. My discussion of these many issues is necessarily brief. For additional information on Freud's views on women (professional and personal) see Gay 1988, 501–22. On the psychoanalytic debate of the 1920s and on Freud and feminism, see Appignanesi and Forrester, 430–74. Edith Kurzweil gives an excellent account of the psychoanalytic debates and of the Anglo-Saxon and French feminists who began to construct a feminism based on psychoanalysis in the late 1960s and early 1970s in *The Freudians: A Comparative Perspective* (New Haven and London: Yale University Press, 1989), 152–72. See also her *Freudians and Feminists* (Boulder, Colo.: Westview Press, 1995). For a view of the subject by a feminist and a psychoanalyst, see Juliet Mitchell, *Psychoanalysis and Feminism: Freud, Reich, Laing, and Women* (New York: Vintage Books, 1974). For attempts to develop a concept of female identity formation, see Carol Gilligan, *In a Different Voice: Psychological Theory and Women's Development* (Cambridge: Harvard University Press, 1982); and Nancy Chodorow, *The Reproduction of Mothering: Psychoanalysis and the Sociology of Gender* (Berkeley: University of California Press, 1978).

17. The issue of the universality of the Oedipus complex remains important for some anthropologists as well as psychoanalysts. See Melford E. Spiro, *Oedipus in the Trobriands* (New Brunswick and London: Transaction, 1993); Johnson and Price-Williams, 3–103; and Wallace, 208–13.

18. See, for example, the paper by psychologists Martin Daly and Margo Wilson, "Is Parent-Offspring Conflict Sex-Linked? Freudian and Dar-

winian Models," *Journal of Personality* 58:1 (1990): 163–87. See also the response to this paper by Slavin and Kriegman, 117–20. Parent-offspring conflict theory postulates universal intergenerational conflict for all sexually reproducing species.

19. Note that it is the content of the anxiety (an erotic or hostile impulse, say), not the affect, that is unconscious. For Freud, as he says in "The Unconscious," there are no unconscious affects or emotions (*SE,* 14:177–79). One way of understanding the goal of psychoanalysis is that it attempts to reunite an affect with its correct idea (the father, for example, rather than a horse).

20. Freud argues here explicitly against Otto Rank's thesis in *The Trauma of Birth* (1924) that anxiety is based on a visual memory of the trauma of birth. For Freud, only general sensations are possible at this time. He sees Rank's idea as unfounded and improbable. But his own view of the experience of birth as a preparation for anxiety is equally speculative.

21. On this point, see Ellman, 225–81.

22. For Allen Esterson, all of Freud's cases involve unfounded construction based on theoretical preconceptions and suggestion. See *Seductive Mirage: An Exploration of the Work of Sigmund Freud* (Chicago and LaSalle, Ill.: Open Court, 1993), 35–93. Like other recent critics, Esterson also argues that Freud manipulated the data of his cases to create what he wanted.

23. For an interesting discussion of this controversy, see John Forrester, *Dispatches from the Freud Wars: Psychoanalysis and Its Passions* (Cambridge: Harvard University Press, 1997), 208–48; hereafter cited in text.

24. See the chapter on personal memory (especially the section on autobiographical memory) in Brown, Scheflin, and Hammond, *Memory, Trauma Treatment, and the Law,* 116–39. I have not addressed the question of whether all past significant memories survive. Freud believes they do. Many memory researchers do not.

25. Freud here reverts to an analogy first suggested in the 1907 essay "Obsessive Actions and Religious Phenomena." The analogy is based on the resemblance of obsessive and religious rituals. In *Moses and Civilization,* Robert Paul takes this analogy seriously in his interpretation of the Judeo-Christian tradition.

26. Not all psychoanalysts agree with Freud's critique of religion; nor do all agree that psychoanalysis requires atheism or religious skepticism. See, for example, W. W. Meissner, S.J., M.D., *Psychoanalysis and Religious Experience* (New Haven and London: Yale University Press, 1984) and Stanley A. Leavy, *In the Image of God: A Psychoanalyst's View* (New Haven and London: Yale University Press, 1988). For a theologian's response, see Hans Küng, *Freud and the Problem of God,* trans. Edward Quinn (New Haven: Yale University Press, 1974). On Freud and modern theology, see Peter Homans, *Theology after Freud: An Interpretive Inquiry* (Indianapolis: Bobbs-Merrill, 1970).

27. Freud uses civilization and culture interchangeably.

28. Other methods include identification and aim-inhibited love relationships, restrictions on love, the commandment to love one's neighbor as oneself, the violence of the law against criminals, and the abolition of private property (as in Russia) so that the hostility of the unpropertied will disappear—none of them, in Freud's view, effective against aggression.

29. Strachey translates Freud's *Unbehagen* in *Das Unbehagen in der Kultur* (the German title of this book) as malaise, but I prefer unrest.

30. As in Fyodor Dostoevsky's *Crime and Punishment* (1866), which Freud must have read (among other works of Dostoevsky) in preparation for his 1928 essay "Dostoevsky and Parricide." Freud greatly admired Dostoevsky as an artist and psychologist, but not as a moralist.

31. Freud agrees that "a real change in the relations of human beings to possessions" would help, certainly more than an ethics of control, but not if it is based (as it is for the socialists) on a "fresh idealistic misconception of human nature" (*SE,* 21:143).

32. *The Letters of Freud and Arnold Zweig,* ed. Ernst L. Freud (New York: Harcourt, Brace and World, 1970), 91–92; hereafter cited in text as *Freud-Zweig.*

33. On Freud and Moses, see Jones 1957, 3:367–69; Gay 1988, 605; Erich Fromm, *Sigmund Freud's Mission: An Analysis of His Personality and Influence* (New York: Grove Press, 1959), 80–84; and Irving E. Alexander, "If Freud Were Moses," in *Personology: Method and Content in Personality Assessment and Psychobiography* (Durham and London: Duke University Press, 1990), 133–75.

34. Ilse Grubrich-Simitis also makes this point in "Freud's Study of Moses as a Daydream: A Biographical Essay," in *Early Freud and Late Freud,* trans. Philip Slotkin (London and New York: Routledge, 1997), 53–89.

35. Later, in Christianity, it emerged in a disguised form in the sacrifice of Jesus (the son) for God (the father).

36. On Freud and Sellin, see Yerushalmi, 25–27.

37. Freud's word is *Geistigkeit,* which Strachey translates as intellectuality. The alternative, Strachey says, is spirituality, which in English arouses "very different associations" (*SE,* 23:86 n). Strachey obviously wants to avoid any theological implications.

Chapter Six

1. J. Bernard Cohen, *Revolution in Science* (Cambridge: Belknap Press of Harvard University Press, 1985), 352; hereafter cited in text.

2. Lear, however, argues that reasons are causes and that an acausal hermeneutics is only one version—and a wrong one—of this approach. See Lear, 49 n.

3. Because critics such as Grünbaum see the same methodological problems in both, I make no distinction here between Freud's and contempo-

rary psychoanalysis, which for many analysts has developed far beyond Freud's original theories.

4. On neuroscience see Laurence Miller, *Freud's Brain: Neuropsychodynamic Foundations of Psychoanalysis* (New York: Guilford Press, 1991.)

5. *Models of the Mind,* ed. Arnold Rothstein, M.D. (New York: International Universities Press, 1985), studies seven different models. Whether the proliferation of these models or schools represents creative ferment or, as Fancher argues in *Cultures of Healing,* a "Culture in Chaos" is open to debate (130–38).

Selected Bibliography

Primary Works

The Complete Letters of Sigmund Freud to Wilhelm Fliess, 1887–1904. Translated and edited by Jeffrey Moussaieff Masson. Cambridge: Belknap Press of Harvard University Press, 1985.

The Freud/Jung Letters: The Correspondence between Sigmund Freud and C. G. Jung. Edited by William McGuire. Translated by Ralph Manheim and R. F. C. Hull. Cambridge: Harvard University Press, 1988.

For Freud in German, see *Gesammelte Werke.* Edited by Anna Freud, Edward Bibring, Willi Hoffer, Ernst Kris, and Otto Isakower. Vols. 1–17. London: Imago, 1940–1952. Vol. 18 and one unnumbered supplementary volume, Frankfort am Main: S. Fischer Verlag, 1968, 1987.

Letters of Sigmund Freud. Selected and edited by Ernst L. Freud. New York: Basic Books, 1960.

The Letters of Sigmund Freud to Eduard Silberstein, 1871–1881. Edited by Walter Boehlich. Translated by Arnold J. Pomerans. Cambridge: Belknap Press of Harvard University Press, 1990.

The Standard Edition of the Complete Psychological Works of Sigmund Freud. 24 vols. Translated under the general editorship of James Strachey in collaboration with Anna Freud, assisted by Alix Strachey and Alan Tyson. London: Hogarth Press, 1953–1974. For Freud's collected papers alone, see *Collected Papers.* 5 vols. Translated under the supervision of Joan Riviere. New York: Basic Books, 1959.

Secondary Works

Biographies

Clark, Ronald W. *Freud: The Man and the Cause.* New York: Random House, 1980. A readable and well-researched book by a British journalist and scientific biographer.

Ferris, Paul. *Dr. Freud: A Life.* Washington, D.C.: Counterpoint, 1998. A British biographer's lively analysis of Freud's life and work. Those interested in current controversies about Freud's life as well as work will find this book of interest.

Gay, Peter. *Freud: A Life for Our Time.* New York, London: Norton, 1988. The most recent complete biography of Freud. Gay—a historian by training—draws on much new biographical material and also addresses the many controversies about Freud's life and work that have raged since the publication of the Jones biography. The long bibliographical essay is invaluable.

Jones, Ernest. *The Life and Work of Sigmund Freud.* 3 vols. New York: Basic Books, 1953–1957. For many years, the authoritative work on Freud's life and work, the Jones biography has recently been attacked as overidealizing and biased in terms of its view of early psychoanalysts whom Jones disliked. Though the criticism is true, the book is still essential for students of Freud.

Newton, Peter M. *Freud: From Youthful Dreams to Mid-Life Crisis.* New York, London: Guilford Press, 1995. A very detailed study of Freud's intellectual and emotional development from birth to the end of the 1890s. Newton uses Freud's letters to Eduard Silberstein, Wilhelm Fliess, and Martha Bernays as developmental records of the several adult transitions in Freud's life during his formative years.

Freud's Vienna and Austria

Barea, Ilsa. *Vienna.* New York: Knopf, 1966. A readable and comprehensive history of Freud's city by a native Viennese.

Crankshaw, Edward. *The Fall of the House of Habsburg.* New York: Penguin Books, 1969. A valuable and readable work on Freud's social and political world in the late nineteenth and early twentieth centuries.

Johnston, William M. *The Austrian Minds: An Intellectual and Social History, 1848–1938.* Berkeley: University of California Press, 1972. This book delivers exactly what its title promises—a comprehensive examination of Austria's intellectual and social world of the years covered. It contains three excellent chapters on Freud and psychoanalysis and one on Hungarian psychoanalysis.

McGrath, William J. *Freud's Discovery of Psychoanalysis: The Politics of Hysteria.* Ithaca and London: Cornell University Press, 1986. Argues that Freud developed intellectually, not as an isolated scientist searching for truth, but under the influence of the Viennese political and intellectual life of his youth and early manhood.

Morton, Frederic. *A Nervous Splendor: Vienna, 1888/1889.* New York: Penguin Books, 1980. A portrait of Vienna in the 10 months leading up to the suicide of Crown Prince Rudolf. The cast of characters include members of the court, writers, painters, musicians—and, of course, Freud.

———. *Thunder at Twilight: Vienna, 1913/1914.* New York: Scribner's, 1989. A portrait of Vienna in the 20 months prior to the assassination of the

Archduke Franz Ferdinand at Sarajevo. In addition to Freud, Adolf Hitler, Leon Trotsky, and Joseph Stalin are all in Vienna during this period.

Schorske, Carl E. *Fin-De-Siècle Vienna: Politics and Culture.* New York: Knopf, 1980. A study of Vienna's cultural and political life at the end of the nineteenth century.

General Works

Appignanesi, Lisa, and John Forrester. *Freud's Women.* New York: Basic Books, 1992. The women of this book are Freud's patients and psychoanalytic colleagues. Biographical material on both is subtle and interesting. Discussion of the theoretical work of the women analysts is substantial. The final chapters on theories of femininity in psychoanalysis from Freud to the present are immensely useful.

Bergmann, Martin S. *The Anatomy of Loving: The Story of Man's Quest to Know What Love Is.* New York: Columbia University Press, 1987. A survey of Western ideas of love, of Freud on love, and of subsequent psychoanalysts on love.

Bucci, Wilma. *Psychoanalysis and Cognitive Science: A Multiple Code Theory.* New York: Guilford Press, 1997. A complex and rewarding effort to rethink Freud as a cognitive theorist.

Crews, Frederick. *The Memory Wars: Freud's Legacy in Dispute.* New York: New York Review, 1995. A representative volume in the anti-Freud crusade of this former Freudian.

Donn, Linda. *Freud and Jung: Years of Friendship, Years of Loss.* New York: Scribner's, 1988. A useful analysis of the rise and fall of a famous friendship.

Drinka, George Frederick. *The Birth of Neurosis: Myth, Malady, and the Victorians.* New York: Simon and Schuster, 1984. Written for a popular audience, this book contains a wealth of information on the evolving concepts of nervousness and neurosis from the eighteenth century to the time of Freud. Deals with the doctors, their theories, and the patients they treated.

Ellenberger, Henri F. *The Discovery of the Unconscious: The History and Evolution of Dynamic Psychiatry.* New York: Basic Books, 1970. A comprehensive study of the development of the concept of the unconscious from the late eighteenth to the end of the nineteenth century. Contains substantial chapters on Freud, Jung, Alfred Adler, and Pierre Janet. An indispensable work.

Fancher, Raymond E. *Psychoanalytic Psychology: The Development of Freud's Thought.* New York: Norton, 1973. A useful introduction to Freud's work containing an especially good exposition of the *Project for a Scientific Psychology.*

Fine, Reubin. *A History of Psychoanalytic Thought.* New York: Columbia University Press, 1979. A useful one-volume history of psychoanalysis.

Grubrich-Simitis, Ilse. *Back to Freud's Texts: Making Silent Documents Speak.* Translated by Philip Slotkin. New Haven and London: Yale University Press, 1996. A study of Freud's surviving manuscripts as they evolve from notes to drafts to firm copies. The book also contains a valuable history of Freud editions and thoughts on future editions.

Grünbaum, Adolf. *The Foundations of Psychoanalysis: A Philosophical Critique.* Berkeley: University of California Press, 1984. One of the central works in the current debate on Freud by a philosopher of science who challenges the scientific status of psychoanalysis.

Kardiner, Abram, and Edward Preble. *They Studied Man.* New York: Mentor, 1967. A study of 10 thinkers (one of them Freud) who contributed to the development of anthropology in the late nineteenth and early twentieth centuries.

Kurzwell, Edith. *The Freudians: A Comparative Perspective.* New Haven and London: Yale University Press, 1989. A sociologist's survey of the organization, reception, and development of Freud's ideas in the United States, France, Germany, and Austria. An important book for anyone who wants to understand national variations in psychoanalysis.

Lear, Jonathan. *Love and Its Place in Nature: A Philosophical Interpretation of Freudian Psychoanalysis.* New York: Farrar, Straus and Giroux, 1990. A philosopher's meditation on the meaning of love as Freud describes it—or as he should have described it. A very subtle, quietly critical reading.

MacMillan, Malcolm. *Freud Evaluated: The Completed Arc.* Cambridge: MIT Press, 1997. A comprehensive analysis and critique of every phase of Freud's work attempting to show that Freud was wrong in virtually every aspect of his theoretical and clinical work.

Masson, Jeffrey Moussaieff. *The Assault on Truth: Freud's Suppression of the Seduction Theory.* New York: Penguin Books, 1985; reissued with a new preface under the title *The Assault on Truth: Freud and Child Sexual Abuse.* New York: Harper Collins, 1992. Contends that Freud was wrong to abandon the seduction theory, that he knew it was correct, and that he was a liar and a coward in making this decision.

Miller, Laurence. *Freud's Brain: Neuropsychodynamic Foundations of Psychoanalysis.* New York: Guilford Press, 1991. An attempt to use the findings and concepts of contemporary neuropsychology through which to examine Freud's ideas on hysteria, dreams, and parapraxes. Requires some knowledge of neuroscience.

Mitchell, Stephen A., and Margaret J. Black. *Freud and Beyond: A History of Modern Psychoanalytic Thought.* New York: Basic Books, 1993. A good introduction to developments in psychoanalysis after Freud.

Neu, Jerome, ed. *The Cambridge Companion to Freud.* Cambridge: Cambridge University Press, 1991. A varied and interesting collection of essays on aspects of Freud's work by scholars from a number of different disciplines.

Rieff, Philip. *Freud: The Mind of the Moralist.* New York: Anchor Books, 1961. A brilliant exposition and critical analysis of virtually every aspect of Freud's work.

Ritvo, Lucille R. *Darwin's Influence on Freud: A Tale of Two Sciences.* New Haven and London: Yale University Press, 1990. The only book-length study of Freud's debt to Darwin. Especially valuable in questioning the common assumption that Freud was a Lamarckian.

Roazen, Paul. *Freud: Political and Social Thought.* New York: Knopf, 1965. A valuable and comprehensive study of Freud as a social and political thinker.

———. *Freud and His Followers.* New York: A Meridian Book, 1976. A study of Freud's many followers throughout his life, much of it based on interviews with still-living participants in the development of psychoanalysis.

Robinson, Paul. *Freud and His Critics.* Berkeley: University of California Press, 1993. A largely successful defense of Freud against three of his major critics—Adolf Grünbaum, Jeffrey Masson, and Frank Sulloway.

Slavin, Malcolm Owen, and Daniel Kriegman. *The Adaptive Design of the Human Psyche: Psychoanalysis, Evolutionary Biology, and the Therapeutic Process.* New York: Guilford Press, 1992. Attempts to build a bridge between modern evolutionary theory and psychoanalysis. Requires a good grasp of both theories.

Spector, Jack J. *The Aesthetics of Freud: A Study in Psychoanalysis and Art.* New York: McGraw-Hill, 1972. The most comprehensive study of Freud's works on art and the artist ever published.

Sulloway, Frank J. *Freud, Biologist of the Mind: Beyond the Psychoanalytic Legend.* New York: Basic Books, 1979. A long and fully (too fully) detailed study of Freud's intellectual roots in various elements of nineteenth-century biology. The book's anti-Freud bias is muted but clear in the implication that Freud is far less original than commonly supposed and that he borrows deeply from Wilhelm Fliess. Sulloway is more openly anti-Freud in his recent book *Born to Rebel: Birth Order, Family Dynamics, and Creative Lives* (New York: Pantheon Books, 1996).

Wallace, Edwin R. *Freud and Anthropology: A History and Reappraisal.* New York: International Universities Press, 1983. Written by a medical historian, this book surveys all of Freud's works that relate to anthropology, discusses these works in the light of anthropology of Freud's day, and evaluates them in the light of contemporary anthropology.

Webster, Richard. *Why Freud Was Wrong: Sin, Science, and Psychoanalysis.* New York: Basic Books, 1985. Argues that Freud was a messianic personality who founded a pseudoreligion that should now be unseated to allow a true science of the mind to develop. In spite of this thesis, there are many important issues (such as, did and does hysteria actually exist?) raised in this book.

Winson, Jonathan. *Brain and Psyche: The Biology of the Unconscious.* Garden City, N.Y.: Anchor Press/Doubleday, 1985. A fascinating attempt by a neuroscientist to construct an account of Freud's unconscious on the basis of contemporary neuroscience.

Wollheim, Richard. *Sigmund Freud.* New York: Viking Press, 1971. The reading of Freud is subtle and complex. There is an especially good chapter on Freud's ideas on neurosis. Long after its publication, this book remains one of the best introductions to Freud.

Index

The Author

Richard W. Noland is professor of English at the University of Massachusetts at Amherst. He received an M.D. from Emory University and a Ph.D. in English from Columbia University. He is a past chairman of the English Department and has held a number of other administrative positions in the university. For one year he was an exchange professor at the University of Freiberg in Germany. He has taught graduate and undergraduate courses on psychoanalysis and literature and has published many articles on this subject. He is also the author of articles on a wide range of subjects including medicine, film, and American Western fiction.

The Editor

David O'Connell is professor of French at Georgia State University. He received his Ph.D. in 1966 from Princeton University, where he was a National Woodrow Wilson Fellow, the Bergen Fellow in Romance Languages, and a National Woodrow Wilson Dissertation Fellow. He is the author of *The Teachings of Saint Louis: A Critical Text* (1972), *Les Propos de Saint Louis* (1974), *Louis-Ferdinand Céline* (1976), *The Instructions of Saint Louis: A Critical Text* (1979), and *Michel de Saint Pierre: A Catholic Novelist at the Crossroads* (1990). He has edited more than 60 books in the Twayne World Authors Series.